I0407816

Before the Book:

Tips on publishing, marketing, and networking to build your brand

Before the Book:

Tips on publishing, marketing, and networking to build your brand

Traci M. Sanders

Copyright ©2017 by Traci M. Sanders

All rights are reserved. No part of this book may be reproduced by any mechanical, photographic, or electronic process, or in the form of phonographic recording nor may it be stored in a retrieval system, transmitted, or otherwise be copied for public or private use—other than for "fair use" as brief quotations embodied in articles and reviews without prior written permission of the publisher.

The author's intent in providing this book is to offer tutorial advice on topics related to the writing and publishing industry. Any book references or links, or name references, have been agreed upon by the original owners of this content.

Table of Contents

Introduction   11

Publishing your book   13

TIP 225: 7 mistakes authors make when publishing   15

TIP 227: Can I use this in my novel?
(content permissions)   18

TIP 228: The price is right – or is it?   21

TIP 229: A rose by any other name … pros and

Cons …   24

TIP 230: Reel 'em in (creating hooks for your book)   27

TIP 231: 9 things to consider when
creating your book cover   29

TIP 232: Choosing cover images for your books   32

TIP 233: Mastering your manuscript   35

TIP 234: How to write a query letter   38

TIP 235: Taking the fear out of writing blurbs   42

TIP 236: 10 things I learned about publishing a book 46

After You Publish Part 1

Marketing Your Book   49

TIP 237: Know your audience – part 1 – children's

books and middle-grade fiction   51

TIP 238: Know your audience – part 2 – YA fiction   55

TIP 239: The 3-month rule (when to start promoting

your book)   57

TIP 240: Reach and teach, but try not to preach   60

TIP 241: Language barriers can affect authors and readers   63

TIP 242: Places to advertise your FREE book, or your book for free   66

TIP 243: Free is not always a good thing   69

TIP 244: Affiliate yourself with Amazon   73

TIP 245: The fame game (success by association)   76

TIP 246: Save time with these links   77

TIP 247: Every day is a holiday (marketing all year)   80

TIP 248: Name dropping in your books   85

TIP 249: Making money as a creative (aside from book sales)   88

TIP 250: Sway your readers with swag   92

TIP 251: 19 things to do to ensure a successful book signing   95

TIP 252: How to become a best-selling author   100

TIP 253: Making money writing magazine articles   104

TIP 254: From the lips of readers (What makes a reader one-click a book?)   106

TIP 255: It's a group effort   109

TIP 256: Theme parties for your books!   110

TIP 257: Personalize your book giveaways   113

TIP 258: What to do after a book signing   114

TIP 259: Writing for a cause can expand your fan base   117

TIP 260: Building your brand with an e-mail signature   120

TIP 261: Do you make your books easy to buy?   122

TIP 262: Take your readers/followers with you   124

TIP 263: Making a book perma-free on Amazon   125

TIP 264: How to draw a crowd at a book signing   127

TIP 265: Automation is not always a good thing   130

TIP 266: Becoming famous in your hometown   133

TIP 267: Building an email list   135

TIP 268: Your books in action (book trailers)   137

TIP 269: Music to my eyes (soundtracks to your
stories)   139

TIP 270: Giveaways that work!   141

TIP 271: Homegrown sales –
(marketing your books locally)   143

TIP 272: Creating calls-to-action for your books (and
blogs)   147

After You Publish Part 2

Networking to Build Your Brand   149

TIP 273: Don't get sucked into social media   151

TIP 274: How often should you post on social media?   153

TIP 275: Managing multiple social-media accounts   154

TIP 276: Staying on schedule online   157

TIP 277: The adult version of tag   159

TIP 278: Is a picture worth a thousand words?   161

TIP 279: Hashing out #hashtags   164

TIP 280: Make a list and tweet it twice.
(more tips on Twitter)   167

TIP 281: Addressing readers' concerns and questions   169

TIP 282: Taking over Facebook (all about takeovers)   171

TIP 283: Live readings … to build your fan base   174

TIP 284: Online groups for authors   176

TIP 285: Social media etiquette   180

TIP 286: Engage your Twitter audience with a Q & A
session   184

TIP 287: Networking with local authors to
build your fan base   186

TIP 288: Making the most of Goodreads   188

TIP 289: Ten ways authors can strengthen the Indie
industry   191

TIP 290: Ten ways to "pay it forward" as an author   194

TIP 291: Oops! Your human side is showing.
(connecting with fans personally)   197

TIP 292: Expanding your audience by guest blogging   198

TIP 293: Re-purposing and re-blogging content to build
your following   200

After you Publish Part 3

Building Your Brand Through Blogging   203

TIP 294: Do I really need a blog/site?   205

TIP 295: Website or blog?   207

TIP 296: Creating your "about me" page   210

TIP 297: Tips for successful blogging   214

TIP 298: 9 ways to trim blog-post creation time   218

TIP 299: Blogging about your books
(increase exposure and sales)   220

TIP 300: What to blog about … besides books   223

TIP 301: Quality vs. quantity – don't short change
your readers   227

TIP 302: Book bloggers and authors (a match made in
book heaven)   229

TIP 303: 3 types of virtual blog tours   233

TIP 304: No comment (blogging etiquette for readers) 237

After You Publish Part 4

All About Reviews 241

TIP 305: 7 reasons why friends/family don't review
your books 243

TIP 306: Resources to encourage more reviews for
your books 246

TIP 307: How to handle low-star reviews (and
why 5-star reviews aren't always best) 251

TIP 308: How to write solid Amazon reviews 257

TIP 309: Reviews aren't just for books 260

After You Publish Part 5

Genre-Specific Marketing 263

TIP 310: (For romance authors) 13 tips on writing
love scenes 265

TIP 311: Just what is considered clean fiction? 269

TIP 312: All about the kids 273

TIP 313: 7 tips for children's books that rhyme 277

TIP 314: Marketing to young children and teens 280

TIP 315: How short should short fiction be? 283

TIP 316: Short treasures – more on short pieces 286

TIP 317: Tips for multi-genre authors 295

TIP 318: 11 ways to keep your stories going (sequels) 297

After You Publish Part 6

Managing the Media 301

TIP 319: How to build an author portfolio – media
package 303

TIP 320: Public speaking   305

TIP 321: Capitalizing on media appearances   307

TIP 322: Tips for radio interviews   309

TIP 323: How to get on TV   312

Conclusion   317

Special thanks   319

Introduction

In 2016, I hosted a daily segment on my blog *A Word With Traci* (www.awordwithtraci.com) in which I offered tips on various aspects of the publishing industry. Most of these tips were aimed at Indie authors, but some applied to traditionally published authors as well.

The topics included writing, editing, publishing, and marketing.

Now, you can have all these tips in the palm of your hand, broken down into three easy-to-follow guides that cover specific stages of the publishing process:

Before You Publish (Volume I): Tips on grammar, writing, and editing

Beyond The Book (Volume II): Tips on publishing, marketing, and networking to build your brand

Living The Write Life (Volume III): Tips on making the most of your writing skills

Whether you have been in the publishing game for decades, or you are just getting started on this unpredictable-but-thrilling ride, you are sure to discover some new ideas in these books that will help you along on your writing journey.

* * *

This book offers tips on everything that occurs in the publishing process, and beyond—publishing, marketing, and networking. You will find unique tips to market your book and network with fans and fellow authors. This book follows Volume I in this three-book series.

So, dive in, bookmark the tips you like, and discard the ones that you don't need. I'm happy to answer any questions or address any topics you feel aren't covered in this series. You may email at tsanderspublishing@yahoo.com.

Thank you for taking the time to read my books. I wish you much success in your own publishing endeavors!

Publishing your book

TIP 225: 7 mistakes authors make when publishing

Readers, and authors—especially first-time authors—often have no clue what goes on before the "publish" button is clicked, or perhaps what *should* occur.

As many authors will tell you, writing the book is the easy part—comparatively speaking, anyway. Editing, designing, formatting and choosing the right fonts, marketing, etc. That's where the real work comes in. Perhaps because it has gotten so easy for people to click that *publish* button, no matter what the book reads like or looks like, a vast number of sub-par titles have been released in the past few years.

These tips will help ensure your book doesn't fall into that category.

Here are 7 mistakes new authors make: (this is only involving the publishing aspect, not the writing)

1. Not hiring a professional editor. Think of your writing as "the middle" of the process, instead of the beginning. With most foods, the best part is the middle. Oreos, cupcakes, jelly doughnuts, etc. Let's take a cupcake, for instance. The cake is usually the true reason people eat it, but if the icing leaves a bad taste in our mouths, there's a good chance we may never even get to the cake. Right? Consider professional editing the icing on the cake.

2. Not hiring a professional cover designer. Unless you are proficient in Photoshop, InDesign, or some other high-quality design program, leave this task to the professionals. A good book cover can cost anywhere between a couple hundred dollars to a few thousand. It all depends on who

you chose, what images you use (stock or custom), and the detail involved. But considering that cupcake again, even if the icing tastes amazing (great editing), your audience may decide not to risk it simply because the presentation is sloppy (the cover).

3. Not having a budget set. This is a huge part of an author's profitability. It's a good idea to do your research before publishing, sometimes even before writing your book—to know what you are getting into. It's quite easy to blow a budget on cover design and editing alone. You still have marketing to consider. That is where most authors drop the ball. They spend a fortune to get the book in perfect shape (editing and cover-design wise) and have no funds left for marketing.

4. Exhausting their budget on the wrong marketing strategies. It's easy to find those $25-for-one-week-of-Tweets promotions, and the like. They are all over social media. But which one is right? Which one will give you the biggest ROI (return on investment)? That is where research comes in. Word of mouth is going to be your biggest ally in this endeavor. Ask your author friends what promotions have worked for them. Check reviews for the company. And go with your gut. Think outside the box as well. If you see a marketing strategy and want to put your own unique spin on it, plan it out and go for it. Readers love uniqueness.

5. Waiting until the book has released to begin marketing for it. If it's one thing I've learned by connecting with successful Indie authors, it's that marketing for your book begins before you even start writing it, if you plan to have success, unless you have a huge marketing budget to play with. You must begin building a buzz about your story before you finish writing it. Get your readers excited about the characters and story line through teasers, trailers,

updates on your story, and personal video connections. Stay connected to your readers! Offer ARC copies to certain readers so they will have reviews ready to post on the day of your book release.

6. Not knowing your genre or target audience. I've met several authors who've asked me to determine their book's genre. It was quite confusing, especially when that person's book wasn't my usual cup of tea. Authors need to know their genre so they can find their target audience. Learn where your readers hang out, online and off. Learn what type of book swag they like and what type of characters they are drawn to.

7. Not choosing a catchy title and/or blurb for the book. Titles can make or break a book's success. If the title is too short or ambiguous, readers are confused as to what the story is about, and may not take a chance on it. If it's too long and cumbersome to read, or say, they may also avoid it because they won't be able to remember it to share it with their friends. Even with a great title, if the blurb falls flat, readers won't even take the time to dive into the sample.

I could list a host of others, such as, loading too much front matter in the book, not offering a professional author bio and picture, and choosing stock images that have been overused. But those aspects are not as crucial as the seven I listed above. There are many elements to consider and manage before you publish. Take time to research these things, and learn from others' mistakes. Be wise!

TIP 227: Can I use this in my novel?
(content permissions)

As an author, I have come across this situation many times – wondering if I can include a certain website link, song title, etc., in my novels.

This can be a touchy subject, since novels (relatively speaking), have income potential. Therefore, due royalties for creative property may become an issue, in some cases.

Here is a short list of things authors CAN include in novels (published works), without having to obtain permission from the creators:

- work that is public domain (most works published before 1923 are considered public domain, and some even all the way up to before 1964)

- (common knowledge) facts – naming things such as the Declaration of Independence, or copying a list of all the US presidents, etc.

This includes items such as song titles, book titles, TV shows, artist names, etc.,

It is NOT OKAY to use song lyrics, book or movie lines, web content, or poetry lines without explicit permission, as that is copyright infringement.

- Nursery rhymes, the Alphabet song, and Finger-plays are all public domain.

- Linking to websites – this does not cover copied content, only the links.

- When you abide by "fair-use" guidelines, meaning, the majority of the content you provide is originally yours. Only small portions of others' works may be used.

What is fair use?

Fair use is basically any copying of copyrighted material that is intended for educational or informational purposes. This applies to music, photography, and software downloads, as well as written works.

Here are a few fair-use scenarios:

- An author including a website link "for more information" in a novel or blog post.

- A student using a photo or music soundtrack from the Internet, for a school project.

- A student quoting a line from a Shakespearean novel, for a school essay.

- An author naming a celebrity, and the movie in which he/she starred, as part of a novel.

**Be aware that just because it's on the Internet, does not mean it's fair-use content!

While there are no hard-and-fast rules for content copyright, some people will attempt to sue others over even the smallest infringement. Therefore, if you have any doubt, it's best to contact a copyright lawyer or research the national copyright laws before including anything that isn't legally yours.

One of my blog followers had this to add about this topic:

The convention in copyright law is the use of "quotes" such as a few lines of song lyrics are okay if they are attributed (not who had the hit with them, but who wrote them), if they tend to stay in the range of around twenty words max, and if they are supplemental to the content rather than central.

An interesting exception to this is that titles cannot be copyrighted, so you can blatantly steal others' statements for use in or as titles. Thus, you can write a novel about a pair of '60s singers and title it *The Beat Goes On*.

Of course, the overarching factor is whether or not the copyright-holder might practically feel aggrieved or perceive you are profiting off another's words. Many are happy to have a few lines or a quote in a book with proper attribution. Thanks, Traci.

Stephen Geez

TIP 228: The price is right – or is it?

This tip is all about digital (Kindle) books. Many elements go into publishing a book, and I've already covered several of these in previous tips, but one thing that can make or break book sales is pricing—too high or too low.

I've seen several Indie Kindle books priced at $6.99 or higher recently and have to wonder what those authors' sales look like. Most of these books have very few reviews, but the ones they do have are quite good.

Perhaps these authors have some inside information on book sales that I don't but, as a reader, I would rarely pay more than $4.99 for a Kindle book, unless it was by an author whose work I'm very familiar with—celebrity or not, or perhaps a self-help book that offers tutorial content.

After being in the publishing business for a few years, reading tons of books by Indie authors, and connecting personally with many successful authors, I have taken notice that the average price of a Kindle book is $3.99. I personally haven't discovered many that are priced at $4.99 or higher.

Also, from connecting with several reviewers and book bloggers, I firmly believe that the main reason a $3.99 book price works best is because avid readers typically read many books in a month and must budget for that. Therefore, most of them aren't able to pay higher than $3.99 for any one book. If it's a title by their favorite author, they may splurge.

On the other end of the spectrum, they steer clear of books priced at 99 cents simply because they fear it's not well written— again, unless they have already enjoyed a book by that author.

And most tend to pass over books priced higher than $4.99, simply for financial reasons.

There are several things to keep in mind when pricing your Kindle book:

1. Your target audience – are they children? (meaning, parents are buying the books). Are they broke teenagers? Struggling college students? Are they lonely housewives or househusbands looking for an escape, probably hiding the Amazon bill from their spouses? (these readers tend to spend the most, by the way).

2. The average price for Kindle books in your genre – You don't want to price it too high to take yourself out of the competition, but you also don't want to price it too low, making your book seem less worthy (or valuable) than others in your genre.

3. You also have to consider what you want your royalty to be. I think many authors price their Kindle books high to be able to recuperate some of their publishing costs. It rarely works this way, unless perhaps the author is a celebrity or has a huge following in place.

4. Your book's topic – is it a specialty/nonfiction book that will offer value to a wide span of people? Books written for authors (about writing, publishing, and marketing tips tend to fare well). Authors can typically price these a bit higher, depending on demand. But fiction is hard to sell when it's priced above $4.99, unless the author is well-known.

5. Consider the page count of your book. If it's a 49-page reference guide, you probably won't do well to charge more than $1.99 for it—again, unless you have a huge following in place, or the content in your book is proprietary. For some reason, readers tend to value e-

books based on page number, especially if they don't know anything about the author before reading it. Therefore, most full-length novels can be priced between $2.99 and $4.99, simply based on quantity.

The good thing about pricing a Kindle book is that you can always change it according to special events or promotions, or if spikes in demand occur, such as if you do a takeover event online and connect with a group of readers, or if you offer your book to a book club. You may want to lower the price to 99 cents for something like that, if a great number of people will need to purchase your book to review it.

After all, like my daddy always tells me: "Collecting 35% of 99 cents is better than 70% of zero."

TIP 229: A rose by any other name ... pros and cons ...

Do you use a pen name? Have you thought about using one? After reading this post, you should be able to make an informed decision about this.

Authors choose to use pen names for various reasons:

1. When they publish books of a sensitive nature and don't want to reveal their true identities.

2. Some authors choose a pen names for certain books and use their real names for others.

3. Some authors use pen names in attempt to avoid tax liability. This can be dangerous and is not recommended.

4. Some authors write certain books under pen names to test the market and see what readers think of their books, just in case they aren't received well.

5. Some authors just want to try something different, write from a different perspective.

Many famous authors use pen names.

Stephen King has written under the name Richard Bachman.

J.K. Rowling published her second book under the name Robert Galbraith.

Agatha Christie wrote romance novels under the name Mary Westmacott.

C.S. Lewis once wrote under the name Clive Hamilton.

Unfortunately, with social media being so invasive and interconnected, true identities can be revealed more easily than they were back during the days of authors like Samuel Clemens. It doesn't take long for the media to discover the true author.

Lesser-known authors often stick with pen names, nonetheless.

Here are some pros and cons of using a pen name:

PROS:

1. It can work well for multi-genre authors, especially if some of the author's books are of a sensitive nature that contradicts his/her usual writing style.

2. An author can disguise his/her true gender. Research has shown that more big publishers entertain manuscripts by white males than any other race or gender.

3. An author can test the waters with a book of a different flavor, without running the risk of tainting his/her brand.

4. Some authors like to hide their identity for personal reasons– familial issues, child-custody cases, or legal issues.

5. Some authors use pen names because their true names are not marketable enough. Publishers often choose pen names for their clients.

CONS:

1. The media is sneaky, and it doesn't take long for an author's identity to be revealed, if the author becomes famous enough. Sometimes fans leak the information.

2. Keeping up with multiple social media accounts can be daunting, expensive, and exhausting. I've known many authors who started out under pen names and wish they hadn't, because sometimes they met fans who they wanted

to connect with personally, and eventually their true identities were revealed anyway; however, since they'd already built a brand with the pen name, they had to keep up with that account as well.

3. If an author doesn't do his/her research to choose a name that doesn't already exist, a law suit could be in his/her future. It's a fine line to walk.

4. In some cases, big publishers are allowed to use an author's real name or pen name as they see fit.

5. An author may unknowingly commit tax fraud.

6. Setting up your royalties can be quite a hassle.

7. Wills can be messy when pen names are concerned as well.

8. If an author's true name is never revealed, how does the author get true credit for his/her work? How does he/she go about doing book signings and media events to showcase the books? The whole point of writing a book is for the author to get *his/her* name out there, not someone else's.

In summation, it can be fun to try a new name in publishing, to play the *Who Am I?* game, but it can be a costly, messy, and tricky game to play. It's a good idea to know the rules and to consider all the possible outcomes before you take on a pseudonym.

TIP 230: Reel 'em in (creating hooks for your book)

Do you want to increase your chances of selling your book? You need a great hook!

What is a hook? It's a short (one-or-two-line) phrase used to market your book. **It's not a synopsis, blurb, or description.** It gives your readers just enough information about your book to make them hungry for more. Even more, a great hook can grab the attention of an editor or publisher and land you a contract. It will be the first impression they have of your story, so it must be compelling.

Here are some quick-and-dirty tips for writing a great hook:

- Write it in first-person POV – it creates a sense of immediacy.

- Never use passive verbs; use strong ones.

- Don't give away too much of the story. Avoid spoilers or revealing too much of the main conflict.

- Keep your main theme in mind – death, romance, loss, grief, coming of age, family, friendship, etc.

- Be passionate about your statement. Make it bold, but don't use too many adjectives or adverbs. Use descriptive nouns.

- Make a small list of the main characters or plot topics, and choose some that stand out to keep in mind when creating your hook.

- Focus on what makes your story unique, and use it to pitch your book.

Here are a couple of hooks which have scored publishing contracts.

Eat, Pray, Love:

After a painful divorce, the author sets out to devote one year to pleasure, prayer and love. She travels to three distinctly different locales to immerse herself in these pursuits. Can a heartbroken and confused woman purposely set out to find happiness?

A Tale of Two Cities:

"It was the best of times, it was the worst of times, it was the age of wisdom, it was the age of foolishness."

I actually have a couple of hooks for my latest romance novel *Unsevered*:

1. Sometimes people are put in our paths ... to teach us how to let go.

2. People say they would give anything to have just one more moment with a loved one lost.

And here is one for my debut novella *When Darkness Breaks:*

A tragedy tears a couple apart. Another one brings them back together. But is it too late to salvage their love?

A hook can be a powerful tool for pulling people in to check out your books. These work well on promo images as teasers, and on social media pages.

TIP 231: 9 things to consider when creating your book cover

In the past few years of researching, I've learned a great deal about the publishing industry.

So far, I've concluded that there are **five elements to the process**.

1. Writing the book

2. Editing the book (including initial edits and final, professional editing)

3. Designing the book cover and copy material

4. Publishing the book

5. Marketing the book

Each step plays a vital role in the success of a book. Professional editors who "get" your story and enhance your words rather than erase them, are worth their weight in gold as far as I'm concerned.

But this tip involves book-cover design. Many authors, due to budget or time concerns, opt to design their own book covers. I'm all about saving money, especially as an Indie author; however, unless you are proficient in special design programs, I suggest hiring a pro for this. And I'm not talking about web designers or even illustrators who "dabble in Photoshop or InDesign." Kudos to them for having those skills, but professional cover design is a whole other creature.

From what I've learned about these programs, they don't compare to the top-quality ones used by the pros. And **print design is much different than web design**, I've discovered.

So, my suggestion is to hire a pro who specializes in print work, even more so, in book-cover design. **A cover can make or break a book sale**. It's the face of your work, the first thing people see that represents you. With more than seven million books on Amazon to choose from, you must make sure your cover stand out.

I personally adore my cover designer. Her name is **Rachel Bostwick**, and she was referred to me by a fellow author friend. She designed both of my book covers and the trailers for both books. I tell everyone about her! In fact, jump on over to her Facebook page to see some of the covers she has designed. Be sure to give her a LIKE while you're there.

You can find her on:

Fiverr.com https://www.fiverr.com/rachelbostwick

Facebook https://www.facebook.com/rachelnbostwick/?fref=ts

Here are 9 things to expect/ask when looking for a professional cover designer:

1. The best advertisement is word of mouth. Ask around with your fellow authors and see who they use. I've already given you one reference.

2. Once you have a few to choose from, be sure to ask to see samples of their work. Check out those covers on Amazon and see how they compare to others.

3. Make sure you know what the total cost will be for everything. A reputable designer will give you a set project price, rather than nickel and dime you to death with fees; and he/she will also give you a reasonable deadline in which to expect your product to be delivered.

4. Be sure to discuss any extra fees that will be involved, if any changes need to be done.

5. Make sure it's clear as to what you can expect for the fee: Does it include just a Kindle cover or paperback also? Does it include a 3D cover? Will you have all rights to use the stock images for other marketing purposes?

6. Make sure your artist has permission to use the stock images chosen for your book. (He/she will probably charge a nominal fee for any images needed to purchase.) Work with your designer to give him or her ideas as to what you envision for your cover. It can be a beautiful process with the right designer.

7. How does your designer wish to be paid? PayPal is the typical method. You will want to choose a reputable designer who can provide a receipt for tax purposes.

8. If you choose someone on Fiverr.com (other than Rachel, of course), or any other design service, be sure to check his or her references to see what the fees and work ethics are like.

9. Make sure the designer guarantees his or her work. If you are not satisfied, you need to be able to get your money back. But keep in mind, any type of design work is time consuming. Respect the designer's time. If he/she does do a great job, don't be unreasonable with changes. Go with your gut if it's not right, but be respectful at the same time.

Those are just a few basic questions to ask/things to consider, when choosing a book cover designer.

TIP 232: Choosing cover images for your books

One thing I've learned about book publishing in the last four years is that covers do help sell a book! The other thing I've learned? A lot of authors use stock images for book covers.

So far, since publishing my debut novella *When Darkness Breaks,* I've seen at least a dozen book covers with the same male model on the front. I recognize him right away. I thought I was being "unique" in my choice. I had no idea how popular he was.

Since publishing my second book *Unsevered,* I've seen the exact same couple used on at least three other covers, and a few promo teasers. This wouldn't necessarily be a big deal, if these images weren't in my same genre but, unfortunately, most of them were.

I personally like to be original, not one to follow the crowd, which makes these discoveries even more disheartening to me.

How does an author avoid clichéd (or overdone) book covers?

Here are a few tips:

1. You don't have to avoid stock images, but choose less-popular ones.

2. When I was choosing the stock models for my romance novels, I went with "pretty and shiny" (eye-catching) versus unique (apparently). Especially if you use a designer from Fiverr or some other book-design company, be sure to check the popularity of your stock image. Google it and see how often it comes up. It's not bad to use stock images, but try to choose intriguing ones or combine a few to create a unique design.

3. You don't have to use the face of a stock model. Depending on your theme and genre, you can opt to use just certain body parts, which are less recognizable.

4. If budget allows, hire a model for your cover. Many art schools and modeling agencies have tons of models willing to do book covers, and some are very affordable.

5. If you do go for the "popularity effect" choose a celebrity model, if your budget allows, or at least an up-and-coming celebrity. I've heard of this resulting in massive payoff for several authors recently.

6. Beware of pre-made book covers that designers sell in bulk. The longer I'm in this business, the more carbon-copy covers I notice. If you do use a pre-made cover, try to choose one with a unique background and a stock model, or vice versa, rather than both. The fonts and colors should follow genre standards, however, for instant genre recognition by the reader.

7. Use other book covers as inspiration, not imitation.

8. Consider buying the rights for specific photos, if your budget allows. Getty Images and Corbis are two sites that offer high-quality photos with rights' management.

9. If you have photographic talent, use it. Perhaps you are skilled at taking amazing photos, but you aren't great with photo-editing programs. Take the photos yourself and hire a designer to edit them.

**It's important to note that while it's a good idea to use "non-clichéd" photos, the themes should follow the genre. Readers detect book genres by their covers.

There are many ways to avoid clichéd book covers. Your options are only limited by your imagination and budget.

Here is a thought on this topic, shared by Stephen Geez:

I design about a cover a week, on average. I'm relying more and more on working with an artist for primary image, a logo renderer for main title, and a feller named Mr. Photoshop for composition. I like how art can provide arresting images, and I'm not limited to available photos and/or models. I like choosing art styles and mediums, too, which are feasible even in digital painting. Point is, stock photos aren't always the place to start because photos aren't always the best choice—though they can be incorporated (see my 2016 re-release of Invigilator). For all-art, compare the 2016 re-releases of Fresh Ink Group Short Story Showcase, What Sara Saw, Zhasou Pure, etc. Thanks, Traci. Covers are VERY important.

TIP 233: Mastering your manuscript

While most of the tips in this book are aimed at authors who choose to self-publish, I do throw a few on traditional publishing in the mix. As well, some authors are hybrids, meaning they choose to publish some of their books as Indies, and list other titles with agents or publishers.

No matter which route you choose, knowing how to format a manuscript is a good skill to have.

First, here are some Don'ts when it comes to manuscripts:

1. Don't use fancy fonts or colors. Your manuscript won't be taken seriously.

2. Don't send your full manuscript unless it's requested.

3. Don't forget to put your name and book title on it.

4. Don't try to reinvent the wheel. Follow the standards.

5. Don't embellish or lie about your experience or talents. Don't claim to be an "award-winning author" if you're not.

6. Don't mention writing accolades or published pieces, unless they were awarded or received from a notable source. (Ex: Don't mention that you had an article published in your local newspaper.)

7. Don't compare your writing to someone famous. Let your writing speak on its own merit.

8. Don't suck up to the agent/publisher by mentioning their work. They recognize it right away.

9. Don't underline anything in manuscripts. Italics will suffice.

Now, here are a few Do's for manuscripts:

1. Do use a 1-inch margin on all sides.

2. Do address a certain agent by name—not "to whom it may concern."

3. Do follow the submission guidelines – only submit what is requested. Don't attach documents if they ask you to copy and paste it into the body of the email. And don't send more, thinking they will "appreciate your work once they start reading." It probably won't make it past the slush pile.

4. Do include a title page, but start the page numbering on the first page of the actual story. It should include: title of the story, approximate word count (to the nearest hundred), author's contact details, copyright details, and agent's details (if represented).

5. Do include a header on each page: your name, title of novel in all caps, and page number.

6. Do start each new chapter on a new page, about one-third the way down the page. Just a side note: most agents/publishers don't want stories with prologues, but if you self-publish, you don't have to worry about that.

7. Do start the first line of the story four to six lines down from the chapter title.

8. Do double space the entire manuscript, except certain lines on the title page. See images above.

9. Do use 12pt. spacing, and Courier font type.

10. Do use left-align for your text.

11. Do single space between sentences.

Whether you are an Indie or traditionally published, it's important to represent your work in a professional manner and have a manuscript at the ready, just in case. Many Indie authors have had their titles "picked up" by publishers at conferences and conventions.

TIP 234: How to write a query letter

Even self-published authors may encounter a need to write a query letter. Whether the author is a hybrid client (meaning, one who has published traditionally but then releases other books through self-publishing), or the author starts out self-published and then decides to look for an agent or publisher.

Knowing how to write a proper query letter is a good skill for any author to have.

The problem is, most authors haven't a clue of how to go about writing one.

Here are a few tips on writing query letters:

1. Always address a specific person, rather than starting it with "Dear Sir or Madam" or the dreaded "To whom it may concern."

2. Learn as much as you can about the specific agent/publisher you are querying. That will show your sincerity and professionalism as an author.
   Ex: I noticed on your website that you are seeking (genre name) titles … and I think my novel (book title) would make an excellent addition to your current list of titles.
   OR
   Ex: I noticed on your website that you represent one of my favorite titles (book title). My current novel (novel title) is comparable in theme.

3. Next, tell a little bit about your title and any accolades it has received, or anything that makes it stand out from the sea of books on the market. Right away, you have to make

the reader care about your character(s) and there must be no question as to what the main character wants to accomplish in the story.

Ex: High -powered news anchor Amber Woods is a thirty-something mom and wife whose perfect life falls apart when, on the way home from dinner one evening, amidst a heated argument, her husband Drake strikes and kills a young boy with the couple's car.

4. The next paragraph should provide further detail, without too much, into the plot of the story.

Ex: Amber eventually moves on, finding solace in her role as a stay-home mom. The family relocates to New York for Drake's new job but the couple learns that their problems can't be outrun as Drake struggles with what *he* did and pushes his family away … until another tragedy strikes, showing him just what he stands to lose.

5. Offer legitimate reasons why your book would be a valuable addition to the publisher's or agent's current list of represented titles. Give the agent or publisher an idea of how marketable your book would be and why.

Ex: This story would appeal to a wide variety of readers, as all humans are touched by death and tragedy at some point in their lives, and they can relate to the hardships this couple faces.

6. Offer the specs of your story.

Ex: This novella is approximately 20,000 words and around 130 pages.

7. In the next paragraph, offer any credentials you have that might help you stand apart from the competition. Don't mention where you graduated high school, or college (unless you have a doctorate or master's degree in a field that relates to your writing or something of that nature).

Ex: I graduated from the Art Institute of Atlanta in 2000

with a master's degree in English and a bachelor's in Creative Writing. I currently have 10,000 followers on Twitter; 6,000 on Facebook; and 2000 subscribers to my blog at (blog address).
{These are not *my* stats, by the way.}

8. Close the letter and thank the person for his or her time.
    Ex: Thank you for your time and consideration of (your book title again). I've included the first chapter, per your request on the site, as an email attachment.
    I look forward to hearing from you. (be sure to follow the website's instructions explicitly)
    Sincerely,
    (your name here)

In this query letter, you accomplish several things:

- You let the agent/publisher know you took the time to learn more about what he/she is looking for specifically in representation. (You respect his/her time and position.)

- You let the agent/publisher know about your book and what to expect in the manuscript.

- You let the agent/publisher know your credentials – why you are qualified to write such a book.

- You let the agent/publisher know what he/she has to work with in media representation of you. (Your established social media following.)

- You let the agent/publisher know that you respect his/her time by following the directions explicitly on how to submit your work.

- And you let the agent/publisher know how to reach you for further details.

A query letter is basically an author's resume for each book he/she wants to publish. Hopefully the tips offered here will help you snag your dream agent or publisher, should you decide to tread the choppy waters of traditional publishing.

TIP 235: Taking the fear out of writing blurbs

This tip is about a topic that can make even the most talented author cringe ... writing blurbs.

It's important to understand that blurbs and synopses are not the same, but they are similar.

Here are descriptions of blurbs and synopses, broken down in simple terms:

Blurb:
a brief, compelling summary of your book which makes readers want to read more. It doesn't include spoilers or the ending. It introduces the main character(s), and describes the main conflict/crisis. This usually appears on the back of a published book to draw readers in.

Synopsis:
a summary of the book which includes the main character(s), the major crisis/conflict, AND a resolution to the problem. It does reveal spoilers and the ending. This is usually a piece of writing that agents or publishers will ask for before considering representing an author. They need to know how the story will unfold and end to ensure the author will be able to provide a salable story readers will enjoy ... and finish reading.

***Synopses apply to manuscripts, whereas blurbs involve published books.

Here are a few tips for writing blurbs.

1. Blurbs are usually written in present tense and introduce at least the main character(s).

2. Blurbs are typically written in third-person POV.

3. Blurbs should be brief but detailed enough to intrigue the reader, making the reader want more.

4. Dialogue is not usually included in a blurb but can be if it reveals something important or exciting about the story. (Ex: It begins with an important quote by a pivotal character, even if the character doesn't speak anywhere else in the book. Such as a mother who died in a character's young life, and whose last words are the motto by which the character lives his or her life. Or it could include a crucial, short conversation between two characters that sets the mood for the story.)

5. Blurbs should present a crisis or a problem to solve.

6. Blurbs usually end in a thought-provoking question to which readers will have an answer by the end of the book.

7. Blurbs should be brief—no longer than a few paragraphs. An author doesn't want to give away too much of the story, and the reader doesn't want to be bogged down with too many details. That's what the book is for.

8. Blurbs should set the tone and mood, revealing the theme and genre for the story: intriguing/suspenseful for mystery; romantic/dramatic for romance; terrifying/unsettling for horror; and so forth for each genre.

I've just offered eight tips on writing blurbs. Many authors shy away from this task, and some don't take the time necessary to make their blurbs the best they can be. But it's important to devote special attention to your book's blurb, as it's likely the first thing readers will learn about your story, beyond viewing the cover.

I personally enjoy writing blurbs because I'm good at short writing pieces rather than full-length ones, hence why I write novellas.

Here are a few thoughts on this topic, shared by my blog followers:

Excellent advice, this. One point you sort of touched on in the last bullet which I'd expand (or make a separate point) is the opportunity for the blurb to show the kind of narrative voice used in the book, too. I like a blurb to sound literary for a literary novel, snarky for something writ wry, metaphoric if that's of stylistic importance, etc. Often I've read a blurb, then seen the book and instantly recognized that someone other than the author wrote the blurb, someone who failed to capture the author's style. A blurb's style can grab me as quickly as its content.

Another point is, I do like the recommendation to end with a question. However, I like to change it up, maybe introducing the question at the beginning and using the blurb to expand and intrigue, or putting the question in the middle, or one of my favorites: penultimately, as in building to a question, then following it with a call to action (that boils down to saying READ THIS TO FIND OUT). Thus: set-up, intro conflict, intro character, draw setting, build scenario, drop in flavor, and … Will Fickle Freddie's fat finger save the world by finding that booger? Follow his ragtag collection of booger-fighting digits as they take on the wildest nostril in the West!

Or something. Point is, I like the question set-up, then the ending that urges potential readers to come find out HOW we get to the answer.

Thanks, Traci. I look forward to my daily thought-provoking tip!

Will tomorrow's post intrigue and expound? Join Traci in her quest to shine literary light into the dark and lonely corners of the

indie author's world!
Stephen Geez

Fantastic post, Traci! The blurb is always hard for me, so I look forward to using these tips for the next one.
Beth Hale

TIP 236: 10 things I learned about publishing a book

At the time of writing this book, I have self-published eight books in various genres. (romance, parenting, children's, and now nonfiction/tutorial) Each book that I released taught me a little more about the industry, my strengths and weaknesses as an author, and relationships with my friends and family.

Here are a few things I have learned since becoming an indie author:

1. Writing the book, for most authors, is the easy part.

2. Some authors edit their own work, and do a great job. But I have learned that professional editing does pay off, and IT'S NOT THE SAME as general (or even college-level) editing. These guys know more about comma splices, fused sentences, correct tense, passive and active voice, and the use of single and double quotation marks than most authors. Most of them became editors because they enjoy the technical side of writing, whereas most authors simply enjoy the creative side. This is not to say that there aren't some excellent author-editor superheroes out there. But chances are, they either received formal training on editing, or they took the time to research the process and became better with each book they published.

3. The cool thing about researching editing tips is, once you learn them, you tend to not forget them, which saves you time and money on future published books.

4. Most authors are too close to their own work, and too emotionally invested in it to be able to edit thoroughly. Many times, it's because they know their story inside and

out, and tend to skip right past common errors – such as passive voice, proper tense, and omitted words.

5. Asking for reviews from friends and family is like asking them to help you move. They love you, and want to help, and even want to be able to come visit you in your new home from time to time (i.e. – read your book); but if it conflicts with their lives or schedule, it's probably not going to happen.

6. Friends and family are not always going to tell you when your book needs work, again, because they love you.

7. Marketing is an everyday endeavor that most authors dread; however, the greater level of online presence and engagement you have, the higher your sales will be. And you will receive more reviews.

8. Success doesn't usually happen overnight, but new connections that lead to success, can!

9. Supporting others goes a long way in the industry. One hand washes another. Eventually, YOU will be the one with clean hands! Until then, you must keep digging in the trenches.

If writing is your dream, just keep at it. Passion tends to be an infectious thing … it eventually spreads to others. If you write what you are passionate about, eventually, you will find others who share your passion!

After You Publish Part 1
Marketing Your Book

TIP 237: Know your audience – part 1 – children's books and middle-grade fiction

Before writing a book of any genre, it's important to know your audience—know their likes and dislikes as far as characters and plots, and know their attention spans.

Middle-grade books would obviously not be as short as picture books, but not as long as traditional novels either. As well, some adult readers might feel cheated by a novella-length romance book.

Here are a few guidelines for children's books, middle-grade fiction, and YA fiction.

Children's picture books:

- Animals are always favorite character types for kids this age.

- A typical picture book is 32 pages, and around 24 illustrations, 500-600 words, no more than 1000, 1-2 single-spaced ms pages.

- Young children respond to faces, especially faces of children their age.

- The words should be challenging enough not to bore the adult who may be reading it to the child, but not overly sophisticated that the early reader can't read it alone.

- Avoid preaching or lecturing, to parents or kids. A subtle lesson on friendship, sharing, or the like is acceptable, if done tastefully.

- Make sure the book has an actual plot, not just words thrown together haphazardly, even if they rhyme. It has to make sense to be memorable.

- Use child-friendly artwork.

- Bad guys never win, if any bad guys even exist in these books.

Early readers – first chapter books for kids:

- Target age is 4-8 years old.

- May or may not have real chapter breaks, could just be small images or large words that separate the sections.

- Typically, no more than 1,500 words, 3 or 4 single-spaced ms pages.

- Font size is smaller than that of picture books, and the verbiage is a bit more challenging to encourage early reading skills.

- Very few images, but the ones present may be black and white rather than color.

- Reads much like a 30-minute television show. The conflict is simple and is solved fairly quickly.

Children's Chapter Books:

- Target age group is 6/7 to 9/10 years old.

- Even more so than in picture books, don't be preachy. Kids this age hate that.

- Between 5,000 and 15,000 words, between 30-40 single-spaced ms pages.

- Very few pictures, if any. If they are funny or sketched images, (cartoonish), they may work.

- Doesn't use adult language, sexually-oriented words, or overly sophisticated verbiage.

- Fantasy, comedy, and mysteries tend to be big sellers in this age group.

- The story doesn't "talk down" to kids this age. Nothing cutesy.

Middle-grade fiction books:

- Target age group is 8-12 (often called tweens).

- No pictures needed, except for cover art, of course.

- Middle-grade fiction can be anywhere between 20,000 and 35,000 words, some even up to 50,000 (for advanced readers), around 40-60 single-spaced ms pages.

- Contain some teen-ish content/language. Perhaps a slang word or two, but no profanity or sexual situations.

- The kids run most of the show in these books, solve their own problems, with very little help or interference from adults.

- Real-life issues are popular in this genre – boy/girl interactions (typically not sex, though), coming-of-age problems (pimples, menstrual cycles, betrayal by best friends, peer pressure, etc.,).

- Kids learn life is not always pretty – child abuse, divorced parents, death of loved ones, during this stage of life.

- Relatable characters and lots of action.

Certain guidelines must be followed if you are writing for traditional publishers, but even if you are self-publishing, it's a good idea to stay within the realm of themes, page count, and structure.

TIP 238: Know your audience – part 2 – YA fiction

This tip concerns one of the broadest genres in writing – YA (young adult) fiction.

Many authors—and readers—don't fully understand this genre. Some think it's targeted to older teens. Some lump it with middle-grade fiction. Others categorize it for eighteen years into the younger twenties.

Here are some characteristics of YA fiction, set by industry professionals:

1. typically 40,000 to 60,000 words

2. Drama and fantasy are popular themes.

3. targeted age group – 12 – 17 (most cap at right before 18, but some adults read YA fiction as well)

4. relaxed grammar. (This isn't to say that authors shouldn't use proper grammar or have a professional edit on their books, but sentence fragments are popular. Also, the dialogue and narration is more relaxed and not as rigid, concerning grammar.

5. egocentric, impulsive, often immature characters

6. non-preachy story themes

7. hashtags and texts, current trends

8. not overly analytical

9. Real-life issues are addressed – sex, drugs, dating, first kiss, puberty, etc.,

10. Often told in first-person POV because teens are egocentric.

11. tends to have more dialogue

12. Adults are not the main characters, and they DO NOT solve the problems for the teens.

YA fiction is one of those genres that can be just as awkward as the teen years. It's a bit too old for "little kids," but a bit too young for some "grown-up" topics. If you're a YA author, or you're considering writing for this genre, be sure to read a lot of YA fiction. Learn the lingo, their mannerisms, their goals and struggles, and what motivates them … especially if you don't have much experience with this age group, because if you get it wrong, these readers can be brutal in their feedback.

TIP 239: The 3-month rule
(when to start promoting your book)

Many authors wonder how far in advance they should begin promoting their books. From all the research I've done in the past two years, the consensus has been ... at least three months. Some even mentioned one year, but I couldn't image doing that with today's reader population. They can barely wait a few days for books they are excited about.

What type of promoting can authors do three months in advance of their release?

Here are some suggestions. Keep in mind, if you set up a release party, make sure your book will be ready in time. I didn't follow all these steps for my first two books, but I wish I had.

Month 1:

Post a line or two from the story.

Post a paragraph (bio) about one of the main characters.

Post the blurb or a hook about the book.

Post a place-holder cover (if your final cover isn't ready) – or get input from your readers about your cover design to get them interested in the upcoming story. Or, schedule a cover reveal – if your cover is ready.

Post images of what you envision your characters looking like.

Send out feelers to build interest. Something like: Who is ready for a sexy cowboy story? OR: Are you ready for the most thrilling ride of your life? OR: Get ready ... in less than 90 days, *Cowboy*

Tears is coming!! Share the title of the story, and your expected release date.

Month 2:

Create a few teaser ads for your story and share one every few days during this month.

Have your cover reveal party, if you haven't already.

Schedule a takeover party on Facebook to give away a couple of advanced copies, with the contingency that they will be delivered when the book releases. Fans like to know they are getting the first few copies.

Share a couple of longer excerpts from your story.

Share a character interview.

Share images of your "characters" on Pinterest, and a little bit of info on each one. You can even go so far as to share images that represent the setting of your story.

Month 3: (release month)

This is the biggest promotion month. The release date is so close, you and your readers can almost touch it.

Hold a countdown until release day. You can even post a calendar that shows the counted down days.

If the story is ready (meaning, it's been through professional editing and final proofing), you can send out ARC (advanced reader copies – PDF or Word) to a few choice people who can go ahead and send their reviews to you to share.

Post something every day about the book – a teaser, an excerpt, anything to build interest.

Set an introductory, promotional price – 99 cents works well for new releases. Give your readers a deadline for this price, such as "just 99 cents for the first 30 days – get your copy before the price goes up on (date)." Build a sense of urgency.

Plan your takeover party and/or release party.

Contact at least ten bloggers who are willing to feature your book release. Readers love hearing about *the next great book* from their favorite bloggers. Try to choose bloggers with high traffic.

Release Day and beyond:

As soon as the book is available on Amazon, remind your ARC people to go ahead and post their reviews on Amazon and Goodreads for you.

Post all over social media that you have a "new release" and continue sharing the links, cover images, teasers, and excerpts. Aim for at least thirty reviews in the first thirty days. That will start your book off with a nice amount of social proof for future marketing. From this point, it's just much of the same.

If it's your first book, it may take a few months to gain that many reviews, but with second or third books, it tends to happen much quicker if you use the 3-month rule for promoting.

TIP 240: Reach and teach, but try not to preach

In other tips in this book, I speak about authors allowing their personal opinions and beliefs to seep into their writing. To a point, this is okay, and even makes for compelling writing; however, one thing that readers do not enjoy is being preached to.

This happens quite often in nonfiction titles, as they are meant to guide the reader or teach him or her something new. Sharing one's experiences or wisdom with others must be done delicately, and not in a way that is belittling or threatening to the receiver.

A reader will quickly close a book if he/she feels a sense of attack or judgment from the author. An author can't possibly know everything about a topic, just because he/she writes a book about it. No one person on this earth knows it *all*. We can only share our personal experiences and knowledge gained from those experiences.

It's okay to offer a hopeful, positive, insightful, or helpful underlying message in your books, but authors must be aware of their tone and word choices.

Another place where this type of writing is often found is within blog posts. Some bloggers/authors use social media and blogs/sites as personal soapboxes. Many times, this comes back to bite them in the end. This is not to say that we can't, as authors, incorporate our personal beliefs and feelings into our stories or blog posts, but they must be woven in delicately and must be presented as integral parts of our writing pieces.

Here are some key words that might trigger feelings of being judged or preached to:

Should

Examples: You should always … You should never …

Alternatives: It's a good idea … It may be best … Based on my experiences, I would highly recommend …

Wrong

Examples: It's wrong to … People who do (x) are wrong … You are wrong in thinking … It's not right to …

Alternatives: Some people feel it's wrong to … Many people have mixed views on … Some will say it's wrong to … I may not agree with … but …

Don't

Examples: Don't do this … Don't do that … Don't try to … (One exception to this rule is in a tutorial book that's offering a specific lists of do's and don'ts.)

Alternatives: Perhaps you could try this instead … It may work better if you …. Another thing you could try is …

I consider this concept with the same merit I give disciplining the little ones I care for each day. If I use the words "don't," "no," "stop," etc., all they hear is the negativity in my voice. If I offer options, they develop problem-solving skills rather than constantly condemning themselves for being "bad."

Therefore, especially if you are writing a nonfiction self-help guide, be sensitive to the feelings of your readers. How would YOU want an author to present this information to you?

Would you keep turning pages if the author were constantly saying, "You're doing this all wrong,"? I'm sure most of us wouldn't.

But if the author said, "Perhaps you didn't know this, but there is a better way to obtain the results you desire, without the struggle," then this phrase would be more attuned to addressing the reader's problem than yelling at the reader for *having* that problem.

Just remember, to convey a subtle message in your fiction novels, you could offer hints within dialogue, or do more showing than telling, to relate how a character is feeling about a topic.

In nonfiction, it's a good idea to stick mostly to the facts and personal experiences to relay information to your readers.

Just picture yourself as the reader, and you should have no problem.

TIP 241: Language barriers can affect authors and readers

I thought this topic might be pertinent to this segment, simply because I've encountered a lot of British authors in my publishing career, some whose books I read and, at first, thought I was discovering typos within because I wasn't aware of the difference between the British language and English language.

One of those differences involves the words *story* and *storey*.

In English, story can mean two things:

1. a narrative

2. a level of a building

The plural of story is stories.

In British, storey means a level of a building. The plural of storey is storeys.

It's important for readers, especially grammar-police type of readers (guilty), to understand that there is a big difference between many words within various languages. We shouldn't be so quick to judge until we have all the facts.

Here are a few other words I've discovered that have VERY different meanings between the U.S. and the U.K.:

Pants:

U.S. – outerwear – a type of clothing that starts at the waist and reaches the ankles on each leg

U.K. – underwear

Braces:

U.S. – a device used to straighten teeth

U.K. – suspenders

Biscuit:

U.S. – a flaky type of bread served with meals

U.K. – a cookie

Trainers:

U.S. – personnel at a gym who help you get in shape

U.K. – shoes worn for running or athletic exercise (sneakers)

Comforter:

U.S. – a thick, fluffy blanket that covers a bed

U.K. – a baby's pacifier

Cider:

U.S. – a non-alcoholic drink made from apples

U.K. – an alcoholic drink made from apples

Knob:

U.S. – a handle on a door or cabinet

U.K. – a penis

Garden:

U.S. – an area used to grow flowers or vegetation

U.K. – a backyard

Rubber:

U.S. – slang for condom

U.K. – an eraser

(Hmm, that could make for interesting romance reads.)

Shag:

U.S. – carpet with long, soft fibers

U.K. – have sex

As you can see, language differs from country to country and meanings within books can be misconstrued. So, authors: make sure of what you're writing before you publish; and readers: make sure of what you're reading before you submit a negative review.

TIP 242: Places to advertise your FREE book, or your book for free

One thing authors are always on the lookout for are FREE places in which to advertise their books online, or places to advertise their free books. I've stumbled across a few, and I'm sharing them here.

As authors know, the more places your book can be found, the more exposure it receives, and a few sales are bound to follow.

Most of these sites require that your book be free during the promotion. Keep in mind, each site has a set list of rules to follow to be able to list your book. Make sure you get signed up during the right time when your book is actually FREE. When doing these promotions, it may be best to make your book free for that entire month so you won't miss a day.

Some of these are forums where you can talk your book up to readers and other authors. Others are places to advertise your book for free.

Also, remember, if your book is free, it will not garner a "verified purchase" on Amazon, for those who are concerned with that. As well, Amazon may decline their reviews.

With that said, here is the list:

1. http://www.kboards.com/

2. https://www.librarything.com/

3. http://www.shelfari.com/

4. http://www.writers.net/

5. https://www.booksie.com/

6. http://www.nothingbinding.com/

7. http://www.bookbuzzr.com/

8. http://www.jacketflap.com/

9. http://www.bookhitch.com/

10. https://www.scribd.com/

11. http://www.whowrotewhat.net/

12. http://www.kindlemojo.com/

13. http://blog.booksontheknob.org/

14. http://addictedtoebooks.com/submission

15. http://www.freebooksy.com/about/

16. http://digitalbooktoday.com/join-our-team/

17. https://www.facebook.com/galleycat/app/362465080506455/

18. http://www.goodkindles.net/p/why-should-i-submit-my-book-here.html

19. http://ereadernewstoday.com/bargain-kindle-books/

20. http://forums.onlinebookclub.org/

21. http://www.bookandreader.com/

22. http://www.reading-forum.co.uk/forum

23. http://www.online-literature.com/forums

24. http://www.writing.com/

25. http://www.ebookstage.com/authorAreaPage.xhtml

It can be quite time consuming to set your book up with each one, but it may result in a few more sales and reviews in the end, as well as accrue a few new loyal readers.

TIP 243: Free is not always a good thing

Many authors, especially when starting out, choose to make their books available for free, in hopes of drawing in readers and reviewers—whether through promotions on KDP or giving copies to certain individuals. But does it work? My answer (opinion) is yes and no. I'll explain.

I've conducted three promotions on Amazon to make my books free, thus far. I've also offered a Kindle Countdown promotion. Out of thousands of downloads and countless hours of promoting my deals on social media, I came away with less than a handful of reviews and almost no subsequent sales as a result. I think I may have figured out why.

Rather than continuing to view these promotions from an author's perspective, I began looking at them *from a reader's point of view*. As an avid reader, long before I was an author, this wasn't too difficult for me. When my most recent promotion ended, I ran an experiment.

Instead of focusing on promoting my books, I began reading like mad. I read books from multiple genres, studied the authors' promotional efforts and methods, and their sales patterns. In this process, I learned some tips on writing page-turning fiction, and what *really* works to increase sales and reviews.

It's a slow-going process but worth it in the end. The secret to gaining reviews and sales of your books is … *helping others first!* Novel concept, don't you think? (See what I did there?)

With the plethora of paperbacks and Kindle books available for readers to choose from these days, the word *free* doesn't really make much of an impact on your target audience. I'm not saying it doesn't matter, or help them choose; I'm simply saying *it's not the only factor they consider* when choosing a book.

So, what *does* make the difference between tapping that *one-click* button and continuing to scroll? Compelling blurbs and hooks, professional book trailers, great promo banners?

Again, yes and no. These things help draw attention to your books, but many authors are creating catchy banners these days. So, what's the number one thing that gets your audience to click that button?

Word of mouth. Simple but true.

Instead of focusing on getting your readers to buy your book, you must focus on building your reputation. As an Indie author, you are not really selling your books, as much as selling *yourself*. You are selling your opinions, thoughts, and values. Most Indie authors are some of the most supportive and selfless people I've ever met. But there are many who are all about themselves—not reciprocating reviews or even mentioning other authors. I do not swap reviews, but I do pay it forward. If someone I've connected with reviews my book, I make it a point to review another author's book within that same time frame, to pay it forward.

You don't have to buy a fellow author's books to support them. You can:

- follow their social media accounts

- follow and comment on their blogs

- re-tweet, LIKE, and share their posts

- send them encouraging/inspiring/funny links or memes

- share important industry info and tips with them when you run across them

- even if you don't read their genre, comment on their covers, trailers, or blurbs

- ask for their input of your covers, trailers, and blurbs – let them know you respect their opinions

- offer to feature them on your blog, or interview them

- even if you haven't read their books, find some of their best reviews on Amazon, and share them

The main reason I feel free books don't always work is, if people have to spend their hard-earned money on something, they tend to appreciate it more.

Many times, unless you have targeted a specific group of people who've agreed to read/review your book, they will not get to it right away. They will continue to read books by authors who have already proven their writing talents, in the minds of these readers.

I will be honest, many times, unless it was a book by an author who I typically read, I've been guilty of downloading free books that I never had the desire to dive into. It's almost as if *knowing it's free makes it less valuable or important.* I can get to it anytime.

In contrast, if I've already read a book by a certain author, and I enjoyed it, I am chomping at the bit to get another one. And if it's free, I feel as if I've won the lottery. *Free books do work—once you have proven your writing skills in the minds of the readers.* They want more!

Another instance where free books work is if an author has one book, perhaps one in a series, that is perma-free, or if it's free for a limited time *if* they buy one of your other books.

One way you can accomplish this without giving your books away? You can write short stories or poems and share them on social media. These are free, to the author and the reader. It doesn't cost the author anything to post these; but, if the writing is compelling enough, it will draw readers in for more. Then they are willing to *buy* your books to experience more of what you represent.

As an avid reader/reviewer, I promote books I like on several social media platforms. In essence, I tell everyone I know about them. Other readers do the same. Keep in mind, a large portion of authors are readers first. So, if you can build lasting connections with these people and promote their work, they will reciprocate at some point in your relationship. It may not happen right away, but it will happen.

And when you see those reviews start coming in—the ones you didn't have to give away a book to obtain—it's the best feeling. Not only do you realize that someone, whom you helped move up the Amazon spectrum in the past, thought enough of you to recommend your work. But you can also take pride in the knowledge that the reader who reviewed your book, actually *chose* to read it, not just because it was free.

Authors spend a great deal of money on covers, trailers, promotional events, and editing. If you don't value your work, why should the readers?

TIP 244: Affiliate yourself with Amazon

This tip is one that one of my dear author friends shared with me not too long ago. I'm talking about – becoming an Amazon Affiliate. It's just one more way to monetize your blog or site.

First, I'll explain how it works; then, I'll go into detail about how to set it up.

When you visit my blog and click on one of the books I have reviewed on Amazon, you will be taken to "my" Amazon page, not just a generic one. Then, while you are surfing on Amazon (still under my affiliate account) and end up purchasing that book, or any other product, I receive a royalty from that sale. Granted, it's not much, but every penny adds up in an author's world—especially Indie authors.

It takes some effort and time to set it up, but once it's configured, you don't have to do it again. And, each time a visitor clicks through an ad or image on your site, cha-ching for you! I've presented the process in steps so you can refer back to this page as needed during the setup.

Now that you know why you need an Amazon Affiliate account, here are the steps to create one.

1. Set up your blog or website. You will need one to participate in this program.

2. Login to your Amazon account and click "Join Associates."

3. Click "Join for Free" and then click "New Customer."

4. Fill in the application fields. Amazon will need your contact information, email address, and bank account information because they will send your royalties to your bank account via direct deposit.

5. Take a look at the features on the Affiliates page. Become familiar with the process.

6. Enter your website URL and information. This is to link your site or blog to the program so that when someone visits your site/blog and then clicks through something on there, they will be "browsing and/or shopping" under your account.

7. Read the agreement and click "Finish." Feel free to include my name in the "How did you hear about us?" field. (smile)

8. Once your affiliate account has been approved, Amazon will send you a confirmation email.

Once your account is setup and you familiarize yourself with the process, you need to link the books on your blog/site to your account. (By the way, this works with other products as well – anything one can purchase on Amazon.)

Go to the backend (admin) area of your blog/site and follow these directions:

1. In the admin section for your post (the post that includes the information for your book, or the one you have reviewed), click on the "Text" section (where the html codes are found).

2. Put your cursor in the spot where you want to insert the image of the book/product you are linking.

3. Open a new window and login to your Amazon account.

4. Search for the title of the book/product you want to link.

5. At the top left of the Amazon product page, you will see a "Link to this page" feature. Click that.

6. From here, you can choose to link to the text and image, text only, or image only. I recommend choosing text and image. Whichever you choose, click the "highlight html" button at the bottom and then click Cntrl+C.

7. Go back to your html code area in your Word Press admin area and click Cntrl+V. This will paste the code into your post.

8. Now click "Visual" to see what your post will look like. If you chose "text and image" you should see your product image with the hyperlink underneath. You always want to include a link because some people buy things from their phones, and images don't always show up. So, at least they will be able to click the link to purchase.

I've just shared one way to monetize your site. Play around with the Amazon Affiliate site and start earning some money for something you are already doing—sharing your books and products you enjoy.

If nothing else, you'll create enough income to at least support your book-buying habit!

TIP 245: The fame game (success by association)

This tip concerns a marketing strategy that may encourage more sales and/or followers to help build your brand. It's called "success by association."

Basically, you find a few well-known books or movies in the same genre as yours and promote them in comparison. Point out some similarities, and be sure to include an image to refresh readers' minds of the comparison title.

Doing this allows an author to use trending hashtags as well, which may draw in a larger, targeted fan base.

For instance, if you write romance or drama, you could promote a Twitter post that says:

Liked the movie GHOST with #demimoore? You'll love *Unsevered* (include link) #amreading #paranormal

Missing McDreamy from #greysanatomy? Try Drake from WDB! (include link) #mancandy #amreading

These are just a couple of ways to promote your books in association with celebrities. You can get creative and come up with your own. The celebrities may even see the post and respond, or better yet ... buy your book! One can dream.

TIP 246: Save time with these links

Authors must maintain a certain amount of online presence each day for many different tasks: marketing to their target audience; connecting with loyal readers; networking with other professionals in the industry; and often querying agents or publishers.

Time is a commodity that always seems to be in short supply; therefore, it just makes sense to maximize your online efforts by taking advantage of shortcuts.

One thing authors can do to save time is create a list of short links to their purchase sites, web pages, blogs, or other social media pages.

There are several free online resources available to utilize for this.

https://bitly.com/ – *(this is one of my favorites)*

http://tinyurl.com/

https://goo.gl/

http://ow.ly/url/shorten-url

http://bit.do/

Most of these sites are quite simple to use by following a few basic steps:

1. Open the web page for which you'd like to shorten the URL.

2. Open one of the links listed above in a new tab.

3. Highlight the URL of the original web page.

4. Click CTRL + C to copy it.

5. Click CTRL + V to paste it in the bar on the "link shortening" page.

6. Now hit ENTER and it will generate a new shortened link for you.

7. All you do from here is CTRL + C and then CTRL + V to copy and paste the new link into a social media post or other document as needed.

By creating a quick reference list of short links to pages you frequently visit (such as in an Excel spreadsheet), you can save a massive amount of time while online, especially when marketing on social media.

**An extra bonus: Short links look neater and more professional on social media posts.

Example:

Some people are put in our paths ... to teach us how to let go. http://www.amazon.com/Unsevered-Traci-Sanders-ebook/dp/B014FWLMQ4/ref=sr_1_1?ie=UTF8&qid=1457308 572&sr=8-1&keywords=unsevered #romance #mustread (and then an image)

This post looks a bit daunting and chaotic.

But if I use a short link:

Some people are put in our paths ... to teach us how to let go. http://amzn.to/1QAxxMm #romance #mustread (and then an image)

It just looks better.

Creating a list of frequently used links will save you a great deal of time in the long run, allowing you to spend your days focusing on what you truly enjoy … writing!

TIP 247: Every day is a holiday (marketing all year)

I've connected with several sales/marketing professionals, as well as read many books on the topic of book marketing. One piece of advice that all of them had in common was, "Focus on what's unique about your product, something that makes it stand out from the crowd."

Marketing any product is an ongoing, time-consuming process. As authors, it can be challenging to find new (unique) methods of promoting our books without feeling as if we are saturating our timelines and feeds with the same "buy my books" themes.

Large companies such as Walmart or Comcast don't worry that their same commercials run twenty times per day and "bother" some consumers. They know that a different audience will see their commercials if they run them at various times. As well, companies such as these know when (during what times) they will reach the largest portion of their target audiences. This is why we see feminine products advertised a great deal during the day or after dinner. (They know that many moms are home during the day watching soap operas, and the ones who aren't, might be catching up on their prime-time shows after dinner—when the kids are settled in bed.)

{By the way, please don't email me or comment below claiming I am stereotyping stay-home moms as TV watchers and nothing more. I know this isn't true because I am a stay-home mom myself. And even though I personally don't watch soap operas or other TV programs during my day, there are a lot of stay-home moms who do. That is why companies target them during those specific times.}

You will also notice a great deal of pampering products being advertised during this time—luxurious perfumes, makeup, bath gels and body washes, etc. These companies also strive to appeal to women's emotional sides through these types of ads. (Example: "You're worth it." by Loreal cosmetics.)

Successful authors are salespeople and must always be selling (or hire someone who will sell for them). We must have information about our products (our books) at the ready, and find innovative ways to convince consumers of what makes our books stand apart from any others on the market.

And just like any other product available to consumers, certain genres of books have seasons in which they will fare better than others. Most boat distributors don't sell as many boats in the winter as in spring or summer. Companies are constantly attempting to work sales and promotions into holidays and current trends. Since authors are essentially small business owners, we should be doing the same.

Here are a few tips on marketing to current trends:

- First, when marketing your books, you MUST stop thinking like an author and start thinking like a reader. Ask yourself, "Where would I hang out if I were a romance (sci-fi, thriller, non-fiction) reader? What is important to me as a reader who enjoys this type of book?"

- If you are a romance writer, there are some key holidays in which you would fare better than others, such as Valentine's Day, during wedding season, or perhaps during the summer months when many are vacationing and catching up on reading. Therefore, you may want to focus your strongest marketing efforts between February and August, since these are key wedding/romance/vacation months.

- For sci-fi writers, you may want to pay attention to local sci-fi conventions, comic book conventions, and scientific shows and market heavily during that season. Or, if a popular movie is releasing around a certain time and your book compares to it, use that.

- If you write thrillers or horror stories, Halloween would be your key time to reach your target audience. Or again, if a new comparable movie or book is released.

- If you are a non-fiction author, you pretty much have open access to readers, depending on the topic of your book. However, people tend to focus on "getting healthy/losing weight/becoming better humans" around New Year's Eve each year, and it continues until the end of summer. Just keep in mind, their interest tends to wane toward the fall and winter as they indulge on comfort foods and baggy or layered clothing. Therefore, they don't put a great deal of effort in becoming "better people."

If you write a novel that has a holiday word in it, such as "Christmas," use that to your advantage and market heavily around that holiday. Many readers are cooped up inside around this time and are looking for a Christmas-themed story.

Here are some other key holidays to capitalize on:

- New Year's: "Looking for a new read for the new year? You might enjoy 'book title.'"

- St. Patrick's Day: Ex: If you are running a price promotion (or free) for your book, offer something like, "Your luck just got better. My book 'title' is free for the week of St. Patrick's Day."

- Valentine's Day: You can market to the "lovers" or even the "anti-lovers" during this month. Ex: "Sick of reading all those sappy love stories? Try my thriller on for size."

- "Looking for a compelling love story that will leave you breathless? Check out 'book title.' On sale for just 99 cents for Valentine's week."

- Easter: "Leave the hunting for the kids this Easter. You've found your next great read – 'book title.'"

- Wedding season: Especially books about brides, romance, babies/family relationships, etc. Again, you can target the "anti-saps" during this season as well if you write titles in complete opposite genres.

- Summer: Beach reads. "Headed to the beach? Don't forget to grab some great reads for the trip. Check out this sizzling romance 'book title.'"

- "Sharks aren't the only dangers you can encounter on the beach. Meet Jack in my new thriller 'book title.'" "There's nothing like a sweet summer romance to complete that perfect beach vacation."

- Fourth of July, Veteran's Day, President's Day, Memorial Day: promote historical fiction, military romances, or military thrillers

- Mother's Day: books about poetry, memoirs, family/relationships, inspirational true stories, etc.

- Father's Day: books about hobbies, working out, sci-fi, crime thrillers, superheroes

- Halloween: thrillers, sci-fi, horror (or anti-books such as these), as well as any given Friday 13th

- Fall: "Fall into your next great read – 'book title.'"

- Winter: Pretty much anything because folks are cooped up inside their homes, hovering around fireplaces trying to stay warm … not motivated to do anything active. Reading is a major hobby during these months.

- Christmas: "Give the gift of a great read this season. Here are some highly recommended titles to choose from." In the spirit of giving around this time, offer titles of your favorite authors to support them instead of your own work. Readers and authors alike respect that.

I just offered a myriad of ways to cash in on year-round promoting for your books. As an author, you have to keep your methods fresh and unique to make them stand out.

**Bonus: Here is a link to a list of other "non-traditional" holidays upon which you could promote your books with a purpose. Click on any given month.

http://holidayinsights.com/moreholidays/index.htm

As a bonus resource, here is a brand new book by my inspirational friend Gisela Hausmann, which includes 100 pitches to media for specific holidays!

https://www.amazon.com/BOOK-MARKETING-Funnel-Including-Pitches/dp/0996897275/ref=sr_1_1?ie=UTF8&qid=148682407 2&sr=8-1&keywords=gisela+hausmann

Happy Marketing!

TIP 248: Name dropping in your books

When using this method of marketing, you must first consider your target audience as far as dominant age and gender. According to the RWA (Romance Writers of America), women make up about 84 percent of romance readers and the typical romance book consumer is between the ages of thirty and fifty-four. Depending on your romance sub-genre, this is most likely your target age group if you are a romance writer. (You can look up the statistics of other genres as well to determine your target audience's ages/genders.)

Now that you know who you are marketing to, you must next consider what other things they enjoy (i.e. songs/musical artists, celebrities, and television shows). **That's how you learn to speak to your specific readers.**

For example: A few twenty-one-year-old females might know who Patrick Swayze is but may not have the same swooning reaction to his name that say a thirty-five or forty-year-old woman would. At the same token, an older woman, of fifty-five or sixty years of age, may not be at all impressed with the name Jon Bon Jovi and may react more emphatically to the moniker Elvis Presley instead.

Name dropping in books can be quite effective to help an author establish a loyal fan base, even if readers don't realize they are being wooed. And when I say name dropping, I don't just mean names of people. I'm referring to songs, other books, movies, actors, actresses, and even cities.

One book series I highly recommend that does the name dropping quite well is the *Abigail Phelps* series by Bethany Turner.

When a reader sees his or her hometown mentioned in a published book, especially fiction, it can be a nostalgic moment. If a reader sees the title of a famous song that he/she adores, there is an unspoken connection formed immediately with the author—many times unknowingly.

I'm an avid reader who has experienced these types of moments. It makes me feel as if I *know* an author better, or that he/she *knows me* better just because we like some of the same things sometimes. It sounds crazy, but it's almost a subliminal form of marketing.

Here are some examples of name dropping for various genres: Romance/Rom-com/Romantic Suspense: (I will share the most about these genres since they are the ones I'm most familiar with.)

Famous love songs—even ones you don't know very well—by artists such as: Percy Sledge, Bryan Adams, Aerosmith, Elvis Presley, Billy Joel, Fleetwood Mac, Elton John, Marvin Gaye, The Beatles, The Bee Gees, Eric Clapton ... the list can go on and on. Try to choose songs that fit your character's age and/or personality. Some characters have old souls.

Famous romance authors: William Shakespeare, Jane Austen, Charlotte Bronte, Emily Bronte, Margaret Mitchell, Nicholas Sparks, Nora Roberts are just to name a few.

Famous Romantic/Rom-Coms: *The Runaway Bride, Pretty Woman, The Time Traveler's Wife, The Bodyguard, You've Got Mail, Notting Hill, Sleepless in Seattle, Footloose, Pretty in Pink, Bridget Jones Diary,* etc. (Did you get a bit nostalgic just reading some of those titles?) I did.

Celebrities: There are just too many to name, but some staples would be Sean Connery, Richard Gere, Tom Hanks, Julia Roberts, Kevin Bacon, Tom Cruise, Nicole Kidman, Sandra Bullock, Pierce Brosnan, John Travolta, Johnny Depp, Daniel Day-Lewis, and so many more names you could drop.

For Sci-Fi and Thrillers: (These are just a few random suggestions. If this is your genre, you will know which names to drop.)

Famous Celebs or Authors associated with this genre: Stephen King, John Grisham, James Patterson, Edgar Allan Poe, Agatha Christie, Peter James, Steven Spielberg, Robert Downey Jr., Daniel Radcliffe, William Shatner, George Lucas, Johnny Depp, etc.

Famous Thriller movies: *Star Wars, Alien, Bladerunner, Jurassik Park, Terminator, The Day the Earth Stood Still, Planet of the Apes, The Matrix, Edward Scissorhands,* anything by Stephen King, Harrison Ford, etc.

For Fantasy: (random suggestions)

Famous Celebs or Authors/movies/books associated with this genre: J.R.R. Tolkien (*Lord of the Rings*), Terry Pratchett (*Discworld*), George R.R. Martin (*A Game of Thrones*), J.K. Rowling (*Harry Potter*), etc.

**Since many actors/actresses play roles in a variety of genres, many of names mentioned above would apply to the Fantasy or Thriller genres as well.

These are just a few suggestions, but I'm sure you get the point. Draw on what you like, what you know, and what's popular for your targeted audience. But try to focus on the timeless classics because trends change. Choose household names of songs, books, and celebrities, and you should do well.

It's important to note that this method must be used sparingly and tastefully to be effective. Otherwise, your book can feel a bit clichéd to some readers.

TIP 249: Making money as a creative (aside from book sales)

Many authors write a book (or multiple books) and focus on **sales only** afterwards, missing other money-making opportunities that could be realized through their writing or other talents.

Book sales are just one avenue of income for an author, depending on his or her talents. If time allows, other lucrative opportunities are readily available for the taking.

Here are 19 alternative money-making endeavors for creative individuals:

1. Podcasts: One way to generate a stream of income with your writing is to offer tutorial podcasts on your blog or site. These work especially well for non-fiction authors. If you have a specialty, you have a money-making tool. For instance, I write parenting/children's books. One of my books is a potty-training guide. I could offer online tutorials (for a price) on potty training. I've successfully potty trained nearly fifty children in my career in child care, so I have the numbers to back up my tips. I would be providing a valuable service for parents all over the world. I also write other types of parenting guides on: how to find the right child care center, and how to get your child ready for school (teaching the basic academic concepts). If you are a seasoned fiction author or editor, you could create a small podcast (seminar) on how to write page-turning fiction. Or you could offer your top ten editing tips.

2. Guest posting on other blogs/sites: The way to make this a lucrative endeavor is to write a great, useful post and include links back to your site for your sales page.

3. Look for writing gigs that pay. You could get paid per article or per word, depending on what company you choose. This not only gives you a bit of extra income, it also helps you hone your writing skills.

4. Amazon Affiliate program.

5. Google AdSense. Get paid to advertise on your blog/site. Visit this link for more information. https://www.google.com/adsense/start/#?modal_active=none

6. Create an audio version for your books. Some readers don't enjoy reading (or fall asleep reading). This allows them to enjoy the story without actually having to do the work. Learn more about these here: http://www.thecreativepenn.com/2014/10/10/read-your-own-audiobook/

7. Make sure to offer your books in digital and paperback format. Readers have different preferences.

8. Offer your books in other languages. Pay a professional translator. Many authors make a great deal of money on these.

9. Join an anthology project online. Collaborate with some heavy hitters by submitting your short stories or poems. Anthologies receive a lot of exposure because they provide a little bit of something for everyone.

10. Schedule speaking engagements at schools, libraries, and local conference locations. If you are a seasoned author and have some valuable tips to share with aspiring authors

or newly published ones, this could be a lucrative endeavor. You can offer advice on: formatting, publishing, hiring professional editors and cover designers, etc. New authors are hungry for information.

11. Offer editing or formatting services on the side. If you've been in the publishing business for a while and you are an avid reader, or great at grammar, you may be able to offer affordable services to Indie authors on a budget.

12. Create and sell cover designs, or social media banners or teasers. If you are artistically inclined with Photoshop or InDesign (or other programs like these), this is a hugely valuable service for authors.

13. If you are an experienced artist/illustrator, you can offer samples of your drawings to children's authors. In fact, contact ME if you are skilled in this area. I write children's books and can't draw a straight line to save my life!

14. Sometimes on Craigslist (example: http://asheville.craigslist.org/) you can find writing/drawing gigs. These are individuals or companies who pay based on the project.

15. If you are talented at writing blurbs or hooks, many authors are willing to pay you to do this for them. This task is one of the most abhorred aspects of the writing business for many of them. I offer this service as well, as I'm much better at shorter passages than full-length novels. It's a way to make a few quick bucks and gain exposure for your writing skills.

16. Become a radio or television guest personality. Once you forge a business relationship with a local station, they will consider you their go-to expert on certain topics if you make yourself available and offer unique advice.

17. You can become a member of www.Fiverr.com where you can set up a vendor account to offer any of these types of services. Content writer, book trailer designer, book cover designer, illustrator, editor, and more.

18. Some local newspapers pay per article for guest posts.

19. Get paid to test products and write reviews for them. Here is a website that offers a few companies: https://elance360.com/product-review/

It takes a bit of time to research the opportunities that are right for you, and of course to write the content; but once you build your reputation, it can't be taken away from you. You are basically selling YOU as a writer, regardless of what you are writing.

TIP 250: Sway your readers with swag

Book swag has become quite popular at book-signing events as well as online giveaways. Some authors like to add a little something extra to their giveaway packages, to build their reputations and make their names stand out in the writing communities.

There are tons of ways to create and implement author swag into your marketing plan. It can be as simple as a t-shirt with the author's book covers on it that the author wears to a signing or other public event. The main purpose of these items is to draw attention to your books and/or your writing in general.

Here are some examples of author swag:

1. jewelry – bracelets, earrings, necklaces, rings, toe rings

2. clothing – t-shirts, sweatshirts, socks, jackets, blankets/throws/pillows, caps

3. paper products/writing tools – bookmarks, post cards, stationary, pens, decals, flyers, posters, business cards, banners

4. food/dishes – personalized candy or candy bars, personalized cupcakes or cakes, coffee mugs, cups, dishes, wine glasses

5. art – sculptures, paintings, candles, framed art, plaques, engraved crystal books

6. personalized – Christmas ornaments, handbags, totes/beach bags, makeup bags, umbrellas, Kindle covers, glasses cases, cell-phone cases, photo buttons, etc.

Typically, author swag is provided by the author about his or her own books; however, sometimes it can work as a gift to another author. For instance, one Christmas I gifted my dearly departed friend Kathryn Treat a lovely personalized crystal ornament of her book. She flipped over it!

Here are a few ways to use author swag:

1. At book signings as bonuses for a purchase of one of your books.

2. At book signings as a raffled item.

3. At book signings as table display items.

4. In virtual giveaways as prizes.

5. In virtual giveaways as bonuses for certain support: following your blog, LIKING your page, subscribing to your blog, etc.)

6. As gifts to other authors for special occasions. Typically, these are personalized gifts of their books, but if they are fans of your writing, you may gift something to represent your books as well.

7. As advertisement for your books. (Ex: I have a charm with each of my book covers on it.) Some authors wear t-shirts with their book covers on them.

8. Posting pics of you with your swag on social media or your blog to advertise your books.

9. Create your own logo for your publishing company or book titles.

Consider adding a little something to your giveaways and book events. You may just be surprised at the increase in sales. All authors offer books (and typically bookmarks or business cards as well). Stand out from the crowd and offer something they will remember.

TIP 251: 19 things to do to ensure a successful book signing

There are many details involved in setting up a book-signing event, but four key aspects can make or break one.

1. Location

2. Timing

3. Weather

4. Author involvement

While you can't do anything to *change* the weather, there are some steps you can take to *prepare for or address* weather issues. Dress appropriately, use pop-up canopies, hold the event inside, and ensure ample parking and a dry entrance to the building.

Before I go any further, let me take a moment to define a "successful book signing." Many authors approach signings with the expectation of selling lots of books, and while this is *one of* the main goals, it's not the only way to measure success.

In my opinion, a successful event occurs when:

1. An author and event coordinator shows up.

2. You have books to sell.

3. Visitors show up.

4. You sell even one book.

Now many of you may be thinking I'm crazy for saying that. But it's important to remember that the purpose of a book signing is not to sell your books. You are there to sell yourself—your ideas and your personality—basically, who you are as an author. You are there to connect with readers (and find new potential readers). For the most part, you will get back what you put into it. I'll explain in the list below.

Here are 19 things to do to ensure a successful signing event:

1. Plan the event at least one to three months in advance, to give yourself time to order books and book swag, and other business materials. Keep holidays, summer vacation, and other events for that venue in mind.

2. Choose an appropriate venue. As they say in real estate, it's all about location, location, location! You need to make sure the atmosphere of the venue you choose goes along with your theme, is a place where potential readers will frequent, and is easily accessible to the public. Visitors on foot will be key, but there still needs to be adequate parking available for automobile traffic.

3. Once the date and location for the signing is set, it's time to get the other details in place. Will you serve food and drinks? Most authors do, if the venue calls for it. Use your own judgement. You don't want to have messy drinks or food around your books, of course, but your guests may stay longer if you provide something to munch on or sip while you talk about your books. Stick to dry finger foods– crackers, chips, raw veggies, and small bottles of clear liquids—water, Sprite, or Ginger ale.

4. Order merchandise at least three weeks (to a month) in advance, in case something goes wrong or shipping is slow. You may want to order business cards or banners, giveaway items/swag.

5. Start promoting right away. Send out "save the date" note cards, and social media reminders about three months before the event, again at one month before, and then about once per week until the event. Adequate promotion is a key factor in the success of your event. You can't rely on local traffic alone. Ask your friends and family to share your flyers and social media posts to help you promote.

6. Gather a few items to set on your table to create an ambiance that matches your book(s) theme. Candles and chocolate are always nice. You'll also want a nice linen tablecloth, if the venue doesn't offer one, to go over your signing table and perhaps one for the refreshments table as well. *If you are conducting your signing at a bookstore, chances are they will not allow food or drinks. But you may be allowed flameless candles or at the very least, a bowl of candy/chocolate.

7. Make sure you have plenty of good pens to use in signing books.

8. You may want chairs to sit in, but don't plan on sitting a lot. You will be standing to greet your guests and to continue conversations with them about your books.

9. Dress appropriately. You will want to be comfortable but not too casual. A nice pair of dress slacks and a button-down shirt for men, and a casual dress, skirt, or slacks for women. Keep jewelry simple but tasteful. Definitely wear anything that relates to your books—pendants, necklaces, charm bracelets, etc. These are conversation pieces. Women: don't wear anything too revealing. You want to be known for your writing, not your body. Wear comfortable shoes because you will be standing a good bit, but not tennis shoes or flip flops. Simple, weather-appropriate shoes will suffice. You can also wear t-shirts, hats, or other clothing that promotes your books. Or you

can wear something that reflects your personality, as long as it's appropriate.

10. Greet each visitor with a smile, and introduce yourself. This is a huge part of the success of book signings—talking to your guests. And don't just talk about *your* books. Get the conversation started by asking if they enjoy reading and what genres they enjoy. If it's your genre, then you can continue talking about your book. Or, you can tell them about your book "in case they know someone who reads your genre." Just remember, you're not there to sell books; you're there to sell *you*.

11. You may want to bring snacks and drinks for yourself, especially if you will be outdoors or not close to a restaurant. If outdoors, you may need sunscreen, a tent, a jacket, etc. (Consider the weather—always check the weather that day.)

12. Make sure you have all means possible for readers to purchase your books. Obtain a Square reader to accept credit-card payments as well as dollars—one and fives—for change.

13. Make sure to have a display stand for at least one of your books (one for each would be better). These allow for a more professional display.

14. Thank each guest who stops by to talk to you. Hand them a business card, teaser card, or a bookmark. Don't let them walk away empty handed. They may prefer Kindle books to paperbacks.

15. If you do a raffle/giveaway, require each guest who wishes to enter your contest, to sign a piece of paper with a name and email address. These can be used later to contact them about your future releases or upcoming signings/events.

16. Bring a friend to help manage the table while you mingle with your guests.

17. Thank your venue host and even consider giving them a copy of your book or some book swag.

18. DO NOT sit at the table and play on your phone when visitors are nearby. This makes you seem uninterested in being there and self-involved. If you are looking something up for a guest, it's fine, but make it brief.

19. Clean up your space completely before you leave. Use the boy scouts' rule—leave it in better condition than you found it. This means no trash or other materials left behind—even the table cloth or table set up, unless the venue director asks you to leave it there.

Keep in mind, each signing you do gives you experience in dealing with people and sales, as well as builds your confidence to talk about your books. So, it's never a waste, even if you don't sell a book. You can't control who shows up or who buys a book. Therefore, take pride in what you can control—your appearance, your confidence, and your attitude.

Happy signing!

TIP 252: How to become a best-selling author

What does it take to become a bestselling author? In this tip, I am dissecting a bestseller on Amazon. Being able to claim bestseller status is a huge honor for an author, especially a self-published one.

As of today, (the date of this post on my blog), the number one bestseller in the romance genre is *Me Before You* by Jo Jo Moyes. But she is a traditionally published author, and I want to focus on a self-published author.

Number three on the Kindle list for romance is *Mister O* by Lauren Blakely. Her bio even proclaims that she is self-published, even though she began her career traditionally published! To date, she has released more than thirty (self-published) titles and is known for writing hot, sexy romance stories that readers can't seem to get enough of.

One would typically expect the #3 title on the Amazon romance list (not to mention and *New-York-Times*-Bestselling-author many times over) to have thousands of reviews, but most of her books have a few hundred reviews, something most of us self-published authors can only aspire to achieve, but still not as many as other bestselling authors.

Here is a recent interview Lauren did about deciding to self-publish three years ago, after being rejected by big publishers.

http://blog.marieforce.com/author-interview-lauren-blakely/

So, what makes a bestseller? A title having the most sales? One would think. But no, it simply means that your title has appeared on any major bestseller list, even once. Of course, everyone knows about the most prestigious list that every author aspires to hit—the *New York Times*.

But … after researching, I found a few more:

Barnes & Noble (BAN)
Publishers Weekly (PBW)
The Boston Globe (BOG)
USA Today (USA)
The Denver Post (DPO)
The Wall Street Journal (WSJ)
The Los Angeles Times (LAT)
WalMart.com (WAL)
BN.com
Amazon.com

The *New York Times* Bestseller list accounts for books sold in brick and mortar stores, so unless your book is placed in those, your chances of making that list are not good. The popularity of certain genres is also taken into consideration. So, you may not have to sell nearly as many books in, say, the humor genre as you would in romance.

Getting on the Amazon bestseller list is probably the most attainable one, since there are so many subgenres now. If your title appears in the top ten of any genre or sub-genre, it can be called a bestseller. It isn't always about how many books the author sells.

Here are some things that Lauren Blakely's books have in common:

1. They all have professional, eye-catching covers.

2. They all have similar, yet different, themes. (i.e. They are all sexy!)

3. They are all priced at $4.99 or less, other than her box series. Even those are less than $10.

4. They all feature sexy models, many showing lots of skin, on the covers. (sex sells)

5. They are all in the same genre. (she writes what she knows and what she's known for)

Now that we know what this bestseller writes, let's learn a bit more about her social interactions and followers.

1. She has over 15,000 followers on Twitter.

2. She has a professional website and she blogs at least once or twice per week.

3. She has a newsletter.

4. She has more than 50,000 Facebook followers.

So, what's her secret?

Well, one can see she's very active on social media and enjoys interacting with her fans. She was persistent in her journey. She has built numerous relationships with bloggers and fans. She found her niche market, and now she writes to her fans' desires and sticks with what she is good at.

Her first book, which became a bestseller, still only has 495 total reviews and has a 4.2 out of 5 stars overall rating.

So, this tells me three things:

1. Not all bestsellers sell the most books.

2. Not all bestsellers are traditionally published.

3. Not all bestsellers have the most reviews.

After doing this research, I firmly believe that reaching bestselling status requires a lot of social media connection with the right people, perseverance, and timing.

One thing that Lauren does is offer pre-sales of her books so that when they do release, they shoot toward the top of the Amazon charts for already having sales. She also gives away ARC copies of her books, which provides a number of reviews ready to post upon release.

I personally haven't read her books yet, but I plan to check them out soon to see if there is something I'm missing, to see what the romance fans truly look for in a book. This is not to say that I plan to switch to dirty romance, but I could probably pick up a few story-structure ideas and see what her calls to action are in the back of her books. You all might want to do the same for your genres.

After learning all this, my advice is to keep plugging away at your writing, but also make time to connect on social media—with fans, with potential fans, and with other authors in your genre. Network, network, network. Your efforts will eventually pay off. It's not always who you know. Sometimes it's who *they* know.

TIP 253: Making money writing magazine articles

For those who are looking to have short stories, poems, articles, or other short pieces of writing published, magazines are a great place to start, for several reasons:

1. Magazine companies usually accept shorter pieces of writing that traditional, large publishers don't.

2. Magazine companies seek real-person interviews and stories, so non-fiction articles and anecdotes are acceptable.

3. Magazine companies often have a smaller slush pile than traditional publishers, as they are genre-specific.

4. Magazine companies can offer a great deal of exposure for your writing, and they can often be stepping stones to the big publishers. You never know who will see your articles and stories.

5. Magazine companies offer a variety of paid writing opportunities, from articles to even product descriptions that pay on a project base.

Having any piece of writing published in a magazine of any size is a huge accomplishment for a writer, but having one published in a literary magazine is an exceptional honor. You can add either of them to your "media room" on your blog/site.

Here is a list of the top fifty literary magazines:

http://www.everywritersresource.com/literarymagazines/

One of my ultimate goals as a writer is to have something published in my favorite magazine, *First for Women*. That would be a huge milestone for my career. I would love to have one of my books reviewed by one of their editors, but I'd settle for a featured article or interview as well.

TIP 254: From the lips of readers (What makes a reader one-click a book?)

Recently, I conducted a bit of research on social media. I posted in several groups online that were dedicated to readers/book bloggers, and asked the single burning question on every author's mind: What is the ONE thing that makes you one-click a book on Amazon?

Is it the cover? The blurb? Word of mouth? Do they only buy if they know the author?

Here are my results: Out of eighteen responses in a couple of days.

REVIEWS:

Carol Corley – "Balanced reviews."

Cynthia Shearer Law – "Balanced reviews for Indie authors, although that has failed me in the past."

Phillip Nork Jr. – "It must be written by an Indie author and have real reviews, not all 5's from friends."

TITLE:

Neha Kumari – "The cover's attractive and if the description at the back is good. Most importantly the title of the book makes it click in one go."

Annette Reid – "If the title and the synopsis grabs me, I'll read that book. I do try to support indie writers for personal reasons."

Tammy Leatherman – "Sometimes the title alone is enough; other times I will skim the synopsis, and if the story idea pulls me in …

SOLD! I don't like to read too much of the synopsis because I like to let a story unfold as I read."

Velma Boyer – "The title and cover of course.no one can drive you crazy if you don't give them the keys. Love that title."

BLURB AND COVER:

Beth Brockie – "The synopsis. I don't go by reviews because there are so many trolls pug there who want only their "faves" to be purchased, so they give bad reviews, sometimes not even knowing what the book is about or the characters' right names."

Jazzica Idamarie – "The Author, the description, and the cover. I think it's the overall package. The reviews matter but don't, even if poor reviews I give it a chance."

Genevieve Scholl – "The blurb for sure."

Amanda Aubrey – "The descriptions are what draw me in. I don't pay any attention to reviews."

Elizabeth Esguerra Castillo – "The prospect of a beautiful story plot which uncovers from page to page. I do read the blurbs and that greatly influence me to buy one."

Haleigh Carlton – "The cover is a quarter of the reason, the other part would be what the description has to say about the book. I think reviews on books are another reason I like one click buys. It's also very easy to click and buy especially when you don't live close to any book stores and you don't want to wait for it to come in the mail."

Isabell Lawless – "I never reads reviews of a book, I read the synopsis and look if the cover is appealing."

Stacie J Green – "I always look at the cover first and then will a little about what the book.is about. However, I have stopped reading all of that, as sometimes it tells too much."

Fionna Hayes – "Am drawn to both Title and First Bite of the Description. If the information provided does not ignite an intriguing lust for more interaction with the plot or characters, the manuscript does not induce further reading …An author must create a ravenous hunger within to become satiated by further exploration … Thank you for hearing my opinion …"

WORD OF MOUTH:

Tricia Davis – "I visit sites like this to recruit new authors books to my e-reader. I'll read what the author has to say and then caching, I buy it."

Shelleyanne Fogarty – "If it isn't one of my authors that I must have, it isn't just one thing, it is a combination: author, book description, price, own rest of series, etc."

So, as you can see, it isn't one certain thing that convinces a reader to purchase a book. It's a combination of elements; however, reviews and blurbs/book descriptions seem to play a heavy role in the decision process. Therefore, it's worth it to spend the time it takes to make those great!

TIP 255: It's a group effort

Aside from books and writing contests, one way to make money and gain exposure for your writing is to participate in an anthology.

This is a book comprised of a collection of short stories or poems submitted by multiple authors. Most anthologies have themes and the submissions must follow those themes. But that can be just the trigger an author needs to inspire a great new piece of work.

I've always written poems and songs, so short stories involved just a bit more writing than that. So far, I've participated in three anthologies in my career. You can find them here.

https://www.amazon.com/RAVE-SOUP-WRITERS-SOUL-Anthology-ebook/dp/B00QVOGEHC/ref=sr_1_1?ie=UTF8&qid=1484416349&sr=8-1&keywords=rave+soup+for+the+soul

https://www.amazon.com/Imperfections-Tipping-Point-Book-3-ebook/dp/B01KZ3EAOI/ref=tmm_kin_swatch_0?_encoding=UTF8&qid=1484416366&sr=8-1

https://www.amazon.com/CROOKED-TALES-Deception-Revenge-Stories-ebook/dp/B01LFP427U/ref=sr_1_1?ie=UTF8&qid=1484416385&sr=8-1&keywords=crooked+tales+traci+sanders

Anthology projects are a great way to connect with like-minded authors, expand your writing skills, and make a little money on the side, though, most times it's more about exposure and branding rather than royalties.

TIP 256: Theme parties for your books!

This tip is all about conducting theme parties to celebrate new book releases or to offer more exposure for your existing books.

Do you all remember the game CLUE, where you had to guess who the killer was? Well, if you write dark fiction, why not create your own Murder Mystery Night event at your local library, high school, etc.?

You can get as creative as you'd like.

Here are a few ideas for the event. Some of these can be applied to all genres.

*distribute flyers in your local town – with an image of your book cover and verbiage that goes something like this:

Enjoy a good whodunnit?
Local mystery author (name) is hosting a live Murder Mystery Party this Friday night at the Civic Center.
Admission is free if you bring a friend! Otherwise it's only $5 per person (this helps cover the cost of your food – if you want to charge something) Or you can say, admission is free and each attendee will be entered into a drawing for a free signed copy of your book. If he/she brings a friend, his or her name is entered twice.)

One lucky person will win a signed copy of (author's name) latest mystery novel (book title).

Finger foods will be served.

Come join the fun!

Food: you probably don't want to serve anything extravagant (or messy) since people will be touching your books. Veggie tray, crackers, and clear liquids will suffice – unless you want to go to the trouble of serving fruit or meat chunks with tiny forks or toothpicks … nothing that requires a spoon or wet wipe! (These rules can be more flexible if you host the event at your own home.)

Music – you may want to have some appropriate music in the background to set the tone for your "surprise reading" of an excerpt of your novel.

Decor – keep it simple, and you may not be able to have much more than a few tablecloths or removable signs – depends on the venue.

Here are a few ideas for theme parties for other genres – all offering a sample reading of your book. You don't always have to tell people you are doing a "book signing." Some of these would work better for your existing group of friends, and others would work well for expanding your fan base.

Parenting/Children's books – a finger painting/craft class – All children (participants) receive a small prize for creating something, but do a drawing for winners of maybe two signed copies of your children's books.

For a parenting guide, you could offer your top three parenting tips and ask moms in attendance to share their worst (funniest) parenting moment via a secret-ballad type of box. You read them out loud and decide the winner.

Horror/Dark fiction – a costume party (especially around Halloween) – have a costume contest. Winner gets a signed copy of your book. Sci-fi/Fantasy – throw an "Out of this World" party – costumes would be cool here too. Decor would make a huge impact for this one – space-related decorations or fairies would be cool. Ask guests to bring an invention or make a homemade robot. Winner receives a signed copy of your book.

Romance – You could have a "Pillow Talk" or "Girl Talk" party with wine and chocolate (for your friends, or if you're feeling bold, you could extend the invitation to the women in your town). It would be similar to a lingerie party. The sexiest piece of lingerie wins a signed copy of your book. Watch a chick flick (rom-com) with your friends and then read an excerpt from your book. Candles and soft music would be an almost must-have at a romance theme party. Maybe even flowers too.

You could play "Name this Rom-Com" where you pull famous lines from movies and winners can receive signed copies of your books.

You could play "Best Date Ever" or "Worst Date Ever" where the women share the details from either type of date. You pick the winner.

Historical fiction or Historical Romance: why not have an adult tea party? Or a Southern Belle dress contest?

These are just a few examples of theme parties (in person) that you can set up as a different approach to reaching fans and maintaining relationships with your current fans. Who doesn't love a party and free food?

TIP 257: Personalize your book giveaways

When hosting a giveaway online – via Facebook, Twitter, on blogs/sites, etc., an appealing and effective way to connect with your readers is to conduct the drawing on a video.

Not only does this offer a more personal approach, it provides a sense of authenticity concerning the drawing. When fans/readers see that you are willing to show your face on camera to send them a personal message and draw the names *right in front of them*, it tends to solidify their faith in you, and it helps you stand out among the other authors who conduct their drawings through written posts on social media.

Scientific studies have proven that humans connect with faces and voices more deeply than with mere words on paper (or a screen), because tone and mood cannot be detected through text only. The shape and position of the eyes alone speaks volumes. They can reveal if a person is being sincere or just feigning interest.

This is just one more way to connect with your fans/readers personally, without leaving your home.

So, slap on some makeup, brush your hair and teeth, and smile for that camera—but remember to be yourself. Be human. That's what the fans/readers care about most.

TIP 258: What to do after a book signing

Congratulations on your first book-signing event! Hopefully it went well and you sold lots of books and made lots of new friends. And even if you didn't, congratulations on living through your first one.

What comes next? That all depends on what you did at the event.

Did you collect email addresses or other contact information from your guests?

If so, be sure to send them a "thank you" email, letting each person know how much you enjoyed meeting him/her. Also, this is your chance to let your guests (hopefully new fans) know about any upcoming releases or in-person events you have scheduled.

Did you rent a booth or table or a spot at a local business establishment for your event?

If so, be sure to send the host a "thank you" card or email to show your gratitude. You may just secure yourself a permanent event location by doing this. Also, clean up your space and return any props or furniture you borrowed.

Do you have books left over?

Hopefully you don't, but if you do, set up a future event or take some of your books to local salons, medical offices, schools, libraries, or any place where people would be waiting for a service (and possibly reading). Leave your teaser cards, business cards, and one or two books, if you're able to. Or you can offer the owner of the establishment a complimentary copy to check out first. Perhaps he/she will even allow you to leave a few on display (or for sale) at the establishment.

If you didn't sell any (or many books) take a few days (or weeks) to research a different venue, or what you could have done differently at this one. A lot of the success of book events depends on weather and timing. If there is another popular event taking place on the other side of town, you may have suffered in attendance because of that.

Did you offer prizes that could be claimed when not in attendance?

If so, go ahead and mail those prizes out promptly and follow up with those people. People like knowing they were *missed* at an event.

Do you have food/drinks left over?

If so, take them home and enjoy them, or donate them to the host of the venue. He/she might appreciate it. Or if the refreshments can be saved for a future event, feel free to hold on to them. Also, be sure to save any paper/plastic goods that can be reused.

Do you have swag left over?

If so, use it for a future in-person event, or use it for online giveaways to draw new fans.

Did you take pictures?

Hopefully you took pictures before, during, and after … especially if you sold books! Fans love to have pictures taken with authors. You should post them on social media, and your visitors can as well.

If you plan to do future events, be sure to save your materials – books, swag, props, table decor, banners and signs, etc. Keep them in good condition for repeated use.

Whatever you do, don't go online and post disparaging comments about the lack of success of your event or "de-friend" those who weren't able to show up. It turns people off to you as a person, as they label you a pessimist or complainer. Enjoy any connections you made and use them to build relationships. Be grateful for anyone who showed up or bought one of your books. And finally, always strive to learn more about the book-signing process and the industry in general, so you can choose the right venue for your event.

Keep writing and sharing your work with others! You'll eventually find your target audience.

TIP 259: Writing for a cause can expand your fan base

Even though most Indie authors never reach celebrity status, if they network effectively, many *are* able to reach (and influence) a lot of people with their words. As I've said before, words have power. Authors hold the key to that power.

One way an author can gain more exposure for his or her books, and do a good deed, is to support a local or online charity and donate a portion of the book sales.

However, there are some rules of etiquette that must be followed, as some charities may not want to be aligned with certain outside projects or brands.

Here are a few tips for contacting charity organizations about donating:

1. Choose a cause that relates to your books or one that you are passionate about.

2. Don't go into the endeavor with the goal of making money; people can see right through that. Approach it with the goal of helping those who need it and raising as much as you can to help them, rather than "selling books."

3. Contact the charity coordinator to make sure it's okay to promote them or mention your name with theirs. The company board may want to check out your book before agreeing to the collaboration.

4. If you want to say something like "20% of proceeds of this book will be donated to a breast cancer organization (or a diabetes organization, etc., – general charities)" then

you don't have to get permission. However, if you name an organization specifically, you may need to.

5. If you have a personal connection with the cause (and a personal story to tell – perhaps your book is a memoir, biography, or autobiography) you might be able to write an article in a publication for the cause (for instance, if the company has a magazine or website). They may even want to interview you to tell your story and share your book.

6. Rather than "selling" your books, you could offer your book to anyone who donates a minimum amount to the cause. Proof of donation will need to apply.

7. Ask permission to use the company's logo or any affiliated images before you promote them.

8. Several websites are available that allow individuals to create personal campaigns to raise funds. The company takes a small portion of the proceeds and allows you to use their brand and website tools.
   https://www.youcaring.com/
   https://www.gofundme.com/
   https://fundly.com/
   https://www.crowdrise.com/

Here are 5 things you should know about fundraisers:
http://www.giveforward.com/p/online-fundraising/fundraising-websites?utm_source=bing&utm_medium=adcenterppc&utm_campaign=_g_fundraising_website

These are just a few things to keep in mind if you are considering donating a portion of your book sales to a charity or collaborating with an organization to raise funds.

I can say from personal experience, it's always best to obtain permission to affiliate yourself with a cause. I was burned by trying to help a woman in my community, I'd never met, who had stage 4 cancer. I wanted to donate all sales from my books for two months to help her family. She thought that since I didn't know her personally, I was trying to exploit her situation. She was angry and depressed because she only had a few more weeks to live. I was trying to help, but she didn't see it that way. Therefore, she sent me a nasty note asking me not to mention any affiliation to her cause. It truly broke my heart because I had planned a signing event where I was about to put the deposit down on a banquet hall and everything. But she didn't know the kind of person I am. She didn't know my true intentions.

So, it's always best to check before you contribute, unless you've already collected the money from your book sales and are ready to write a check. In other words, the organization doesn't have to do anything or even be mentioned in connection with you.

TIP 260: Building your brand with an e-mail signature

Do you have a professional signature for your emails? If not, you should. It's free advertising, without having to utter the words. It's like passing out your business cards, without the cost.

About how many emails do you send per day? Three, four, five? More? And how many email accounts do you use each day? That's how many times your email signature can be seen.

This would come in handy when contacting other authors, bloggers, readers, or even just friends and family. Perhaps you send a party invitation to one of your high-school friends you recently reconnected with. If you haven't told him or her about your writing career yet, this might be a good icebreaker.

You can play around with fonts and verbiage to find just the right signature to represent you. Some fonts may not be available in certain e-mail programs.

Here is mine:

Traci Sanders
Award-winning author of parenting, children's, and romance titles
http://amzn.to/2cYUdKM
~Reviews keep authors writing~

This is a brief way to close an email professionally and let others know you are an author. You can customize it with your own special quote and a link to your work. You can even include your latest tweet.

Below are the steps to create a signature in Yahoo.

From your main Inbox page ...

1. Click on *settings*.

2. Click on *accounts*.

3. Choose the email account you want to apply the signature to.

4. Check the box that says "Append a signature to the emails you send".

5. Format your text and links.

6. Click *save*.

That's all there is to it.

Again, you can play around with the font styles and colors to suit your needs.

Here is a link that explains how to create a digital email signature in Hotmail and Outlook. http://smallbusiness.chron.com/add-digital-signature-hotmail-outlook-email-49219.html

An email signature is a simple, effective way to help build your brand. Don't miss out on this free advertising tool!

TIP 261: Do you make your books easy to buy?

———————✺———————

Many authors follow all the proper steps in their publishing careers—writing the book, employing professional editors, hiring cover designers and formatting specialists, and listing their books on retail sites. But often, one important step is forgotten ... marketing.

I'm not even talking about promoting one's books on social media or paying for promotions. I'm referring to the most basic thing an author can do to market his or her book: promoting it on a personal website or blog.

Too many authors forget this step. They blog faithfully. They promote their books on social media platforms like Twitter, Pinterest, and Facebook. They do radio and other media interviews. But they fail to list their books on their own blogs or websites. And even when they do list their work, they often don't hyperlink their book covers, or offer buy buttons for visitors to be able to purchase their books. In other words, they don't make it easy to buy their books.

Sometimes, a fan (or potential fans) will email and author and say something like, "I went to your blog and it's beautiful. I want to read your book (title), but I didn't see a way to buy it. Is it available on Amazon?" But don't hold your breath for this! Most people will move on at that point. That's why it's important to make your books as accessible and easy to buy as possible.

Here are few steps to take:

1. Create a page on your blog/site that is dedicated solely to your books. It should be named something simple, such as "my books" so that readers have no issues finding your

work.

Multi-genre authors, such as myself, might want to create separate pages per genre for their work.

Here is the link for my parenting/children's books:

http://awordwithtraci.com/category/my-books/

And here are the links to my adult writing: (Each has its own page, which has a summary for the book, a buy button, and reviews posted.)

When Darkness Breaks:

http://www.awordwithtraci.com/wdb/

Unsevered:

http://awordwithtraci.com/unsevered/

2. Make sure your cover images are clean and clear.

3. Make sure to hyperlink your cover images and offer actual links as well, below the images. Some visitors click on images, and others look for clickable links.

4. Keep visitors on your page as long as possible by offering links to your "other works" at the bottom of each individual book's page.

5. Make sure the verbiage on your book's page is neat, has a nice, legible font, and is catchy, like the blurb.

That's all there is to it. List your books on your own website so you have one central place to send your visitors who want to buy them.

You can also offer coupons or special deals for autographed copies (if you have any in personal stock). It's your website, so you can do what you want. Use it to the highest potential to promote and sell, not just your books, but your brand as well!

TIP 262: Take your readers/followers with you

This is just a quick tip about blogs and websites. When creating your page, don't forget to make it mobile-friendly. This is a very important step that many authors overlook or don't realize the importance of.

Thankfully, I have a webmaster who knows all about these things.

If your site is not mobile-friendly, you will most likely lose followers/fans because, in order to view something on an interior link or to view a tab on a page that's not mobile-friendly, the visitor will have to zoom in and out repeatedly to find what he/she is looking for. In this instant-gratification age, this will frustrate a potential follower.

Customers know that most sites offer mobile-friendly viewing, and they have come to expect this feature. Also, Google may not offer your site as high a ranking in search results if it's not mobile-responsive.

Rather than having to scroll left, right, up, or down on a main page, the most important elements are presented, and easy-to-navigate tabs are offered from there.

All my sites/blogs are mobile-responsive because I know that visitors appreciate it and expect it. Plus, I want to keep them on my site for as long as possible.

If followers are frustrated by non-responsive elements, they will move on to another site.

TIP 263: Making a book perma-free on Amazon

Today's tip is all about using perma-free books to build a fan base.

Why would an author spend so much time and money writing, editing, and publishing a book only to give it away? The answer: to build a following for his or her writing.

With the sea of books available all over the Internet these days, readers are all about getting as many free books as they can get their hands on. Granted, if it's a book by a favorite author, a reader will often gladly pay the price, because he/she knows what to expect in terms of writing quality.

But, if the author is unknown to the reader, even a price of 99 cents may seem like too much of a risk. Don't ask me why. Readers buy books based on a few things, as I explained in a previous tip:

1. The author is well known.

2. The author/book comes highly recommended by a personal friend of the reader.

3. The blurb and/or cover is compelling and draws the reader in.

4. The price is comparable to others in its genre, or at least affordable.

Marketing e-books these days is actually a double-edged sword because, on one hand, readers are typically skeptical of a free book written by an author unknown to them, and yet, they expect to receive free or cheap books to read. It's crazy!

But here is the trick: readers don't expect *all* of the author's books to be free. So, one free book is enough to whet a reader's appetite to an author's writing. A perma-free book is good solution to this.

After researching many different ways to make a book perma-free on Amazon, these are the steps I found most popular. This is how I made *When Darkness Breaks* a perma-free book.

1. Publish your e-book on Kindle, but DON'T enroll it in KDP.

2. Publish your e-book at Smashwords.com as well. Make sure your book meets the requirements to be listed in their "Premium" catalog. And make sure you list your book as FREE. For more specific instructions on getting your title listed in the catalog, click here: https://www.smashwords.com/distribution

3. Don't include any Amazon links in the version you submit to Smashwords.

4. Once your book is listed on B&N and iBooks for free, login to your KDP dashboard and send a note to KDP support to notify them that your book is free on the other platforms. Include links for proof and kindly request that Amazon match their price of $0. It has to be listed in the *Premium* section of Smashwords.

That's all there is to it. Within a couple of weeks, your book should list as free on Amazon, and as long as you keep it free on the other sites, it will remain perma-free.

Notify your followers on your blog, social-media platforms, and even inside your other e-books, that ("—") book is free. Many authors use perma-free books as opt-in bonuses on their blogs.

This might work well to draw in more followers if you have multiple titles published, and this book will represent the writing quality found in your other titles.

TIP 264: How to draw a crowd at a book signing

Once you're at a book event, especially one that includes a multitude of other authors, how do you draw attention to *your* books?

One easy way to pull people to your table is to have a slide show playing in the background. Many people are visual and respond to videos and pictures more than writing.

So, while it's great to post reviews or testimonials somewhere on your table, it's also a good idea to either have a collage of photos (preferably one of you with some of your fans who are holding your books), or a slide show of events you've participated in. If this is your first book event, you can always show images of your characters, setting, or other elements of your book, in a slide show.

This gives potential readers an immediate visual of your characters, and the setting of the story. All these things set the tone for the book.

Here are a few other things you can do to draw some attention to your table:

1. Stand to greet guests, and pass out book swag.

2. Play music in the background, to set the tone in the room, or at least at your table. But, make sure it doesn't overpower your voice.

3. Have huge banners in front of, or on the wall behind, your table.

4. Have a themed centerpiece on your table – something unique to draw interest.

5. If the event venue won't allow a big slide-show screen, or you don't have access to one, set up your lap top on the table, with a Power Point playing. Make sure it has sound. Essentially, it's a mini slide show.

6. Have several supporters, dressed casually but professionally, around you for social proof. Not just one person, because you might have the urge to sit and chat with that person, and potential customers might feel as if they are intruding on your conversation.

7. Create a special hashtag for your books/event, print it out on a bright sheet of paper, and display it on the table. You might be surprised who inputs that hashtag into his or her phone and tweets about your event or books.

8. Use nice, sturdy display stands to exhibit your books professionally, rather than simply laying them on the table.

9. Raffles and giveaways work well to draw a crowd.

10. Enlist a team of helpers to circulate the room and pass out raffle tickets or teaser cards (or to simply talk up your books) to visitors in the room, while you stay at your table to greet visitors and potential customers. If you are the only author there, you can have those helpers visit local retails shops or restaurants to do the same, to draw customers in.

Many authors think their only job is to show up, talk to customers, and sign books at an event. But people these days are busy and on the move. Sometimes, we must go to them, rather than waiting for them to come to us. Once we get them, we have to make sure they are enthralled enough by our presentation and personality to buy our books. A little extra effort can pay off in a big way at a book event.

TIP 265: Automation is not always a good thing

By nature, many authors are recluses—avoiding phone conversations, retail lines (we shop online), and "dealing with people," in general. Aside from our fictional *people*, of course. We like them.

However, this lifestyle kills our book sales. ATMs and drive-thru windows don't read or buy books! People do. Therefore, we have to get out and find these people.

This is another out-of-the-box marketing tip. It's really easy to do and won't cost a lot. In fact, if you already have a printer and paper, it will be free, other than the auto fuel it takes you to drive around town. The kicker? It involves going out there … with *them*.

Breathe. It'll be okay.

Here are the instructions:

1. Make an Excel spreadsheet and divide it into about twelve cells. These can be a little smaller than a business-card size. Choose a best line (or small paragraph) from one of your books and type it into a cell. Copy and paste this into each subsequent cell. Or, you can choose various lines. Make sure there are no typos and that the font is legible and visually pleasing. It's best to stick with clean, normal fonts rather than fancy ones. You can also opt to use a card stock rather than flimsy copy paper. Or you can choose a brightly colored paper.

2. Also, put the title of your book from which the excerpt derives, along with your name. You can include your website or Amazon link, if you wish.

3. Print the sheet out and cut out each cell, ending up with small strips of paper.

Now, while you are out and about running errands, keep these strips of paper with you. When you stop for lunch, leave one of these papers with the bill when you pay it.

When you stop by the bank, throw one in the teller's bin with your deposit.

When you stop by the salon, stick a few inside the first page of the top magazines. (And when those stupid post cards fall out, so will YOUR card.)

When you stop by the utility office, leave one with the clerk, if it's allowed.

When you go shop for new shoes or clothes, leave one in a pair of popular shoes.

The options are endless. Instead of handing out business cards or teaser cards, and possibly losing a great deal of money, just leave these. They are small enough to fit into the person's pocket or purse, or be thrown away if the person chooses. But if the writing is compelling enough, you just might get an anonymous sale, or review! You're a writer, so make it good.

Here's an example:
I curl up in a ball under the covers and breathe in what little of him remains on his pillow. Behind my tear-soaked eyes lurks a memory of our last day together when he was alive. It had started out as the perfect day.

Read more of *Unsevered* by Traci Sanders
(available on Amazon and other online book retailers)

Never stop trying new and unique ways to gain exposure for your books. Of course, keep up with the normal paths—Amazon, your website and/or blog, social media sites, etc., but try something that will make a statement and stand apart in the receiver's mind.

I know if I found something like this, I would think, *Now that's pretty creative.* And I would check it out.

TIP 266: Becoming famous in your hometown

No matter how small your town is, there is marketing potential—an opportunity to expand your fan base and gain exposure for your work.

I've discussed several ways to increase book sales locally, so far. This post pertains to another way to become a household name in your hometown: through writing competitions.

Take the time to research writing contests in your state, and enter them. If you win, or even place high enough, you may get a mention in a local newspaper, on the local radio station, or maybe even on local television!

You never know how far the media reach is for the organizations who host these contests, especially if it is a long-standing event in your state or city.

Many times, these organizations offer cash prizes, a publishing contract, or a certificate of some sort. You can share your news of placing or winning, on your blog and other social media platforms, as a credential for your writing.

No matter how small the contest seems, a win is a win, and you should be proud.

Here are a few tips for entering writing contests: (I won't cover them all.)

- Make sure to follow their rules explicitly, as you would when querying an agent or publisher.

- Make sure to send the exact form of entry they request. Most will request a Mobi, PDF, or Word doc.

- Make sure you enter the correct genre and type of writing. If it's strictly poetry they want, don't submit a short story or novel.

- Make sure your title and opening line is catchy enough to grab their attention. These people see hundreds, possibly thousands, of entries in these contests. Make yours stand out.

- Follow the grammar rules strictly, even if you're normally flexible on them in your writing. Do this one by the book. (THE book, not your book.)

- Try to offer a unique piece of writing. Again, something to stand out from the crowd.

- Choose a standard font – Arial 12pt, Garamond 12pt, etc., are safe choices.

- Do not use colored paper, designed paper, colored or fancy fonts on this. Stick with standard black.

- Edit, edit, and edit again. Make sure there are no errors. Read it aloud to yourself or someone else.

- Do the same with your e-mail message when you submit your entry. Make no mistakes in spelling the contact's name, and spellcheck your message as well.

Writing contests are professional references for your work—a resume of sorts. Take your time to research the right ones for your type of writing, and get busy submitting those entries!

TIP 267: Building an email list

This tip involves using e-mail lists to grow your fan base. Since I'm not familiar with this process, I've invited Les Farley, an author friend of mine, to enlighten us a bit on the benefits of using MailChimp to build his e-mail list.

Here is his advice:

My writing is strictly family friendly, so in order to build an e-mail list of only those people, I offer a book of short stories free to anyone who will join my mailing list. As they are signing up, they receive my promise that they will not be spammed. I hold to that promise and only send them messages when I have something new to offer them.

Because I'm building a list of people who are my intended audience, I expect few unsubscribers. I actually shy away from readers who are not my target audience. By connecting with those who most appreciate my writing, trust is also achieved. All ads that I place are directed towards this same type of reader. Reviews will also be kinder because no one is purchasing something that was unexpected. If adult content is something they require, they need not look very far to find it. They'll pass mine up for what they desire and my readers will remain loyal.

I use MailChimp because it's user friendly and has a free version as well as paid versions.

I'm not tech savvy, so any program that I use must be an easy one. Addresses of people who sign up for my mailing list are kept by MailChimp. The email list is populated as the signups continue. There are also lots of YouTube videos for the beginner. It helps so much to see someone using it right before your eyes.

* * *

Be sure to check out Les's books to support him. He writes clean fiction.

https://www.amazon.com/Les-Farley/e/B00GKPVLYI/ref=sr_tc_2_0?qid=1482412642&sr=1-2-ent

Here's a tutorial video on MailChimp. It's easy to follow and implement the steps right away.

https://www.youtube.com/watch?v=tD2xJktE3BU

From what I've heard from other authors, MailChimp is the best way to build a strong fan base; therefore, I encourage you all to take a look at this video and learn more about this tool. I will be doing the same!

TIP 268: Your books in action (book trailers)

There are many tools to help authors market their books these days that weren't available years ago. One of these resources is book trailers.

Just like movie trailers sell movie tickets, book trailers can sell books ... if they are done right.

Any time you can incorporate more of the five senses in describing your books, the higher your chances are of connecting readers to your story. Book trailers incorporate sight and sound (like movies) to draw readers in. Music evokes emotion, and images create a familiarity with the characters.

Here are some important things to remember when creating a book trailer:

1. It's a fact that music affects human mood. Slow tunes can create a sense of sadness or despair while upbeat music can make a person feel happy or hopeful. Choosing the right music for your story is crucial. And if you opt to build your own trailer, you must make sure you choose music that is actually free to use. One resource is http://www.purple-planet.com/ where you can find royalty-free soundtracks. And royalty-free images can be found atwww.pixabay.com/

2. Wording can make or break a trailer. If the story isn't set up well, it won't draw readers in. Spend at least as much time on this as you spent on your book's blurb, if not more, especially if you choose to pay a designer to create a trailer for you, because it's not always easy (or cheap) to go back and fix wording later.

3. If you choose to have a designer create your trailer, be sure you let him/her know exactly what you envision for it, to make sure your story is conveyed correctly–just as you would with your book cover.
   If you'd like a reference, Rachel Bostwick designed both of my book trailers. She can be reached at:
   Fiverr.com
   https://www.fiverr.com/rachelbostwickFacebook
   https://www.facebook.com/rachelnbostwick/?fref=ts

4. Be sure to give credit to any website or person who had anything to do with the creation of the trailer, including stock photo or music sites.

5. Be sure to get an MP4 copy of your trailer to be able to upload to YouTube and share with your readers. Embed the link on your blog and website. Share it on social media to get your friends to like and comment, just as you would your book cover.

To show you just how powerful book trailers can be, here are a few great ones for my friends' books I'd like to share.

Mark Fine - *The Zebra Affaire*

https://www.youtube.com/watch?v=e2t3Dt2b4fc

Stephen Geez – *Papala Skies*

https://www.youtube.com/watch?v=kKoSH3GJKhc

Beth Hale – Magnolia Secrets

https://www.youtube.com/watch?v=e1H2R0pxYHs

TIP 269: Music to my eyes (soundtracks to your stories)

Have you ever read a book and a certain song came in your head? That means you connected with the tone and mood of the story. I do this all the time as a reader. I even have songs in my head when I write certain pieces. Music is powerful, and when it's set to the right words, it's downright compelling. This is one reason book trailers are so effective.

A fun thing authors can do with their stories is to create a soundtrack for them. There are a number of options available to assist authors in this process.

Here are 5 ways to set the tone and mood for your book:

1. Booktrack: This platform is free and offers about 20,000 soundtracks to choose from, or an author can upload his/her own. Otherwise, the company can be hired to handle all the aspects of it for a mere $1000. Yeah, that's a bit pricey for me, but I thought I'd put it out there for those of you with unlimited publishing budgets. This isn't the same as an audio book, as the music does not include verbiage, but you can add sound effects such as rain pouring, heavy footsteps, and more. Find out more about this option here:
    https://promo.booktrack.com/self-publish
    Here is an excellent tutorial on how to use Booktrack:
    https://www.youtube.com/watch?v=iwuIgrRN55c

2. Another thing you can do, which doesn't embed the songs into the book, is create a "suggested listening" playlist and place it at the beginning or end of your digital book. That way, readers can choose if they want to hear background

music or not. You link the music to each corresponding chapter to set the mood.

3. You can also save free mp3 soundtracks and insert them within your books as links. A couple of sites where you can find free soundtracks:
    https://soundcloud.com/tags/ebook%20soundtrack
    http://www.purple-planet.com/
    http://www.freesoundtrackmusic.com/
    https://www.audioblocks.com/royalty-free-audio/music

4. Authors can also create a visual playlist on Pinterest. Basically, you would make a list of suggested songs or soundtracks that readers should listen to when reading your book. This is similar to the "suggested listening" list you'd place at the back of the e-book. Here is a generic playlist:
    http://bit.ly/1pDZ3hG

5. Another tool you can use to create a playlist is Spotify. It's not as popular as Booktrack, which seems to be taking over the e-book soundtrack aspect of the industry, but it's still pretty good, and easy to use.
    https://www.spotify.com/us/

Music can evoke strong emotions in your readers and help them connect to the words more deeply. Isn't that the ultimate goal of every author?

TIP 270: Giveaways that work!

If you have followed along in this book so far, you are aware that I am not a fan of book giveaways—in the sense of making one's book free on Amazon (such as KDP free promotions)—but I am a fan of individual giveaways. I've gained a few reviews by doing this, too!

TWITTER

Since I spend much more time on Twitter than Facebook, I have many more followers there. So, for every 1000 followers I receive, I give away a free e-book. Sometimes it's awarded to my 1000th, 2000th, etc. follower, and sometimes I choose random followers.

I can never have too many Twitter friends, so if you'd like to connect with me there, click https://twitter.com/tmsanders2014 to add me, and *you* might be my next winner!

FACEBOOK:

For every 500 likes I get on Facebook, I giveaway an e-copy of one of my books. So, feel free to jump over to https://www.facebook.com/AWordWithTraci/?ref=hl and throw me a LIKE so I can give away a book.

GOODREADS:

I have conducted one GR giveaway, but I really can't say it was worth my time. I ended up with more than 600 people adding my book to their TBR list; but, we all know how all-consuming that list can be. I didn't even gain a review from the person who won the book. And, I ended up losing $15 on it, with shipping costs.

If you'd like to connect with me on GR to show me a better way, I am happy to learn.

https://www.goodreads.com/author/show/7508333.Traci_M_S anders

Some authors do quite well on Goodreads, but I don't have that much time to spend in the forums and groups. I wish I did. Maybe someday. For now, I'll keep building my follow and LIKE list organically … by begging!! Just kidding.

TIP 271: Homegrown sales –
(marketing your books locally)

Your local area is a great place to get the word out about your books and start building your fan base because these are people who already know you. They know what type of person you are, and most people are willing to support local authors if they are approached in person.

Many self-published authors make the mistake of focusing solely on the big box names to market their work. It's important to remember that these establishments are not the be-all and end-all of book retailers. There are many other lucrative choices. It all depends on your budget, available time, and imagination—as well as the genre of books you are offering.

When considering how and where to market your work, you must first consider the "who" – your target audience. You must think like a reader, which is another great reason to constantly read as an author. Not only does it help improve your writing skills, it also helps you tune in to what readers look for in a book.

To begin with, think locally. Below I've listed some physical (brick and mortar) places to promote your books. I highly suggest you make up some promotional "conversation cards" (as I call them) to aide in this process, since books can become quite expensive and aren't as readily available.

Since I only have two romance novels out at the moment, I was able to maximize my money and space by using a two-sided post card. Each side contains a promo for one of my books.

These are 6" x 14" post cards that have a glossy, professional-grade look and feel to them. They are basically teaser cards you can leave in local, target-rich establishments. You can include your book's blurb, an excerpt, a list of your favorite reviews, or anything you wish to have associated with your books. (I'm happy to share a picture of these cards with anyone who'd like to e-mail me at tsanderspublishing@yahoo.com.)

If your budget allows, you are more than welcome to leave these cards, along with a couple of copies of your books. It may be a good idea to include a note that says, "If you enjoy this story, take the card, but please leave the book for others to enjoy. Thanks." (signed) your name. (or something to that effect)

Here are some genre-specific suggestions of places to target:

Romance/Fantasy:

- salons – hair, nail, tanning

- OB/Gyn offices

- women's boutiques – clothing or jewelry

- teachers' lounges at public schools – if you know a teacher who will set some out for you

- local libraries or small book stores – the big stores like B&N won't usually deal with Indie authors, but the smaller, privately-owned establishments might

- children's boutiques – for the moms who shop there

- adult/novelty stores – for sexy romances and erotica

- children's hobby arenas – such as karate class, dance class, piano class, etc. – some of those parents need something to read while they wait!

- military bases – for the wives, but some men read too

- local hospital on-call room or staff break rooms – if you know a nurse or doctor who can set them out for you

- local dentist's offices – again, for the waiting parents

Crime/Thrillers/Suspense/Sci-fi

- tattoo parlors

- library/local small book stores

- police stations

- fire stations

- music/record store/gaming store

- military bases

- local hospitals – for staff

For some of these places, it would be best if you could leave conversation cards and a couple copies of your books.

YA/Sweet Romance/Clean Reads

- high schools – approach the English teachers to see if they will keep a copy or two in their classroom, or if they will read/review your books to share with the class

- colleges – the same as above

- all salons – hair, nails, tan

- local libraries and small book stores

- local church groups – some churches have book stores and libraries now

Children's Books/Parenting/Self-help

- child care centers

- pediatricians' offices/dentists

- schools/preschools/private schools – even try to schedule a reading of one of your children's books

- libraries and small book stores

- children's boutiques/thrift stores

- vet's office – if it pertains to animals

These are just a few to get you started. Once you take the time to analyze and ascertain who your true target audience is, you will be able to come up with more ways to find and connect them with your work.

The double-edged sword aspect of being an Indie author is that the marketing is completely in your hands.

TIP 272: Creating calls-to-action for your books (and blogs)

This tip is about creating a sense of urgency with your readers. Authors and bloggers need to establish what is known as a Call to Action. This is a statement found at the end of a writing piece, usually involving a link to more information about something. It can be effective at the end of a book, blog post, or article.

Once your readers have experienced your writing, they may be hungry for more; or, they may wish to go tell others how they feel about what they just read. This is why a call to action is important.

This is the call to action at the end of one of my books:

QUESTIONS OR COMMENTS?

My ultimate goal in writing is to tell a good story that evokes strong emotion in readers, with characters that are compelling and authentic. If you feel that I accomplished that goal in this book, I would be honored if you would share your thoughts with others on Amazon.

If you have any further questions or concerns about this book or any of my titles, feel free to email me at *tsanderspublishing@yahoo.com.*

If you haven't already done so, be sure to check out my debut contemporary romance novella, *When Darkness Breaks*

"Reviews keep authors writing!" *TS*

Please share your thoughts on my books at Amazon and Goodreads.

Blog posts and articles can also contain calls to action. After each article or post on your blog, your readers should be left with something to think about, answer, or share. At the bottom of each of my poems, articles, or books on my blog, there is a link which sends the reader to different posts on my blog. (I'm giving all my secrets away here, huh?)

The longer a reader stays on your blog, the higher the chances are of them doing one of three things: sharing your information, buying a product, or commenting on a post or article.

After You Publish Part 2 Networking to Build Your Brand

TIP 273: Don't get sucked into social media

Have you ever planned to sit down and have a productive writing session; but, while you're typing, you see a notification pop up that someone just followed you on Twitter, or Liked your page on Facebook, or posted a new comment on your blog, or ... bought your book and loved it?

It can be a good feeling when these things arise, especially since being a writer is such an introvert-type of existence, at times. But, it can also be detrimental to your writing. You can think you've spent twenty minutes responding to a couple of emails, or liking or retweeting someone's pages or posts, when in reality, it's been two and a half hours!

As they say, time flies when you're having fun.

Here are some tips to help you stay "in the zone" while you are writing:

- Turn the notifications off on your social media accounts, if you have them. You can always turn them back on when you are available—truly available, not just procrastinating.

- Write your stories using a separate computer that doesn't have Internet capability. That should do the trick, right there.

- Put your smartphone in another area, away from your writing space—so you won't be tempted to scan for new emails, likes, or interactions. (interactions=distractions, in this case).

- Choose a writing area that doesn't have other distractions such as television, loud noises, or activity. You may think the park is a great place to write; but, when you see all the dogs running around, or hear the laughter of children, those things may pull you from your writing faster than anything. Those are TRUE human interactions, not just Internet. People crave human interaction on instinct.

- Put a "do not disturb" sign on your door for your family to adhere to. Let them know that they are not to disturb you when the sign is up, unless the house is on fire.

- Set a specific block of time in which you can write. Take breaks when that time is up, to avoid overload. If you have more time later, you can always come back to it.

These are just a few tips to keep your writing on track by managing your time online. Only you know what your limits and tendencies are, so if you're not one who can ignore that red e-mail flag or that instant message popping up throughout the day, your best bet is to work off a computer that doesn't have Internet.

TIP 274: How often should you post on social media?

Today's tip focuses on a question nearly every author asks himself or herself, probably on a daily basis: How often should I post on social media?

How much is too much? How often is too often, or not often enough?

I stumbled across this post when I signed up for Buffer to manage my social-media accounts. It has been quite helpful and has resulted in several followers, retweets, and shares for me already.

Rather than restate everything here, I will offer the link I used. It even has nice graphics to further clarify.

These results and recommendations are based on what top companies using this service have reported about their success.

Here is the link:
https://blog.bufferapp.com/how-often-post-social-media

The longer you use social media, and the more research you do, you will realize that there are key times to post on certain platforms each day, and key phrases to use in those posts.

As Dr. Seuss put it: "The more you read, the more you know. The more that you learn, the more places you'll go."

I live by that philosophy, and it has worked quite well for me so far.

TIP 275: Managing multiple social-media accounts

As an author, it's not always easy to find time to *write* books much less promote them. But it is a necessary part of the publishing process. And the most effective way to reach your target audience is … social media.

The problem is that "social media" is not concentrated in one common location. It's everywhere! Some of the most popular options are Facebook, Twitter, Instagram, Goodreads, Pinterest, Linkedin, and Google+. Then there are lesser-used options like Snapchat, Flickr, Library Thing, Kindleboards, Meetup, Shelfari, and the list goes on and on.

One could spend all day trying to post to each of these groups and/or interact with friends there. That's why it's important to use your time wisely to balance writing and marketing.

Here are 9 things to do to maximize your time online:

1. Choose five to seven (depending on if you want to work five or seven days per week) platforms and designate one per day of the week. (Example below.)
Monday – Facebook
Tuesday – Twitter
Wednesday – Pinterest
Thursday – Kindleboards
Friday – Instagram
Saturday – Goodreads
Sunday – Shelfari
And you are welcome to omit any of these and replace them with double of something else. (Example: Monday and Friday – Facebook.)

2. Check email no more than three times per day – spread out. Make a habit of responding to emails and interacting with visitors on your blogs/social-media pages at the same times each day (or thereabout), so your fans/followers will know when to expect you. It sets a precedence.

3. Do not install social media apps on your phone with automatic notifications. It can be quite distracting. This way you must make a point to go online and login to interact or check messages.

   Create posts to have at the ready for copying and pasting. Include the content, link, and image you plan to use.

4. Schedule posts for social media pages that will allow it, rather than having to physically go online each time. Here is a post about tools that shave hours off social-media time http://www.inc.com/john-hall/7-free-tools-that-will-shave-hours-off-of-social-media-management.html.

5. Don't join too many book clubs or critique groups and overwhelm yourself trying to keep up with "being supportive." Pick two and be as active as your schedule will reasonably allow. Be aware, too, that many of these clubs are filled with people who thrive on drama and complaining—not the kind of people who will help you get where you want to be.

6. Create a collection of images you will likely use for blog posts and social media posts.

7. Also, create posts ahead of time to promote your closest online friends (to cross-promote in networking) so you can copy and paste them to save time. Be sure to tag them in the post.

8. Finally, if your budget allows, hire a social media assistant to manage your posts or promotional events. I know of a

few authors who do this to allow themselves more writing time. And those authors simply pop in at the right times to interact with their fans.

Social media is definitely a necessary evil for authors, but as long as you manage your time wisely, it can be quite an asset as well.

TIP 276: Staying on schedule online

This tip is about a tool I've recently discovered, and I love it! It's called Buffer.

Some of you may already be familiar with this or may even use it. If not, I highly recommend it. It has freed up so much of my online time.

As most of you know, I stay pretty busy between this blog, writing my books, editing on the side, and of course, promoting other authors on my new site Readers Review Room. So, any time I spend online must be strategic.

While I don't recommend using this tool as a replacement for actual interaction with your followers, it can offer a ... well, a buffer in between manual posts.

I chose the $10/month plan to allow more options, but they do have a free plan.

Rather than answering all the questions about Buffer here, you can check out this link to search specific topics you have questions about. This is the plan I currently have.

https://buffer.com/faq/plans-pricing/#what-are-key-features-awesome-plan-vs-individual-plan

Here are highlights I've discovered thus far:

1. My plan allows me to connect up to ten social media accounts at once and offers between three to five posts per account per day. (You can choose how you'd like to spread your posts out between platforms. It offers up to 100 posts at a time.)

2. Buffer has "suggested" times built in to your posts, based on "high-traffic posting times" it detects. But it also allows you to change these times if you want.

3. It's only $10 per month. That's worth my sanity.

4. It's time saving. I schedule all my weekly posts on one day and it takes me about thirty minutes to get them all in, compared to about twenty minutes per day I used to spend. Every minute counts!

5. It condenses your links for you, rather than having to use Bitly or Tiny URL, or other shortening programs.

6. It offers the option to replace your link with a clickable image. That's cool!

7. Most of the time, it will detect the image that corresponds with the link you insert, saving you time of having to attach the image each time.

8. It's user friendly. I didn't have to watch a tutorial or read a web page to start using it.

9. It allows up to fifteen RSS feeds per connected profile.

10. It works! I've checked it several times and my posts go through as scheduled, with all the features I expected within the post.

I do hope you all check out Buffer.com to save time on social media. (I have no affiliation with Buffer, other than as a customer.)

TIP 277: The adult version of tag

Twitter has become a major player in social media, especially for authors. Learning to navigate Twitter can be a daunting task at first. One thing you can do to build loyal followers, and encourage new ones, is play an adult version of "Tag."

Basically, this is a form of cross-promotion. On occasion, instead of tweeting about your own books, products, or websites; you tag a person in a post about their books, products, or websites.

When Twitter members see you supporting others instead of constantly promoting yourself, they will find you by the hashtags or tags and follow you.

Here are some tips for creating cross-promotion posts:

- Make sure to include the author's (or Twitter follower's) handle. (Example: @tmsanders2014) This is essentially "tagging" them on social media.

- Include a short link to that person's book or product sales page, or website.

- Incorporate appropriate hashtags. (Example: for an author, you might suggest a genre-specific hashtag such as #romance. Or it can be one related to a product or website theme, such as #health #writingtips #marketing)

- Include a quality theme-related image or meme to draw attention to the post (Example: an author's photo or book cover, for general product promotion such as health tips, include something like an image of an athlete).

- In the tweet, ask others to follow this person.

Examples of cross-promotion posts:

- Follow author @Anitas_haven for #inspirational posts and #booksuggestions (include a theme-related image – no link needed)

- Get your thrills and chills with "The Threshold" by @Anitas_haven. (Amazon short link) (include book cover image)

Need tips on #writing #marketing #publishing? Follow @tmsanders2014 (include theme-related image – perhaps a typewriter or author writing on paper)

These are just a few ways to support other authors or followers on Twitter—other than just retweeting their tweets on occasion. It's a more personal approach, and they will become loyal followers … and might even buy one of your books or products.

TIP 278: Is a picture worth a thousand words?

There is an old saying that states, "A picture is worth a thousand words." This may be true. Well, for some authors a picture may be worth sixty-thousand words (smile).

If you haven't figured it out yet, I'm talking about the effectiveness of Pinterest in marketing your books. I've sold quite a few books using this site. Why? Because (pulling from the saying above) pictures can replace/represent words sometimes, especially for those who learn or experience things best through visual aids.

Here are a few tips on how to use Pinterest to market your books:

1. Visit www.pinterest.com to open a free account.

2. Just as you would with any other social media platform, search for friends/acquaintances and follow their Pinterest boards. Most of the time they will follow you back. And many times, they will find you before you find them.

3. Start creating a board and title it. A Pinterest board is like a huge bulletin with Post-It notes on it. Basically, it's similar to you flipping through a magazine and tearing out pictures you like and posting them on your bulletin board.

4. The great thing about Pinterest is that, as long as you choose images/ideas within the Pinterest community, you don't have to worry about "copyrights or intellectual rights" when sharing them. That's what it's for. So, you can type in a keyword in the search bar at the top and start

pinning away. As long as you don't try to claim the image or content as your own, you are covered.

5. Once you've created a new board, titled it, and found an image/article that interests you, click "Pin it" to add it to the specified board. You can even add a caption if you'd like.

6. Another way to use Pinterest is by having your readers upload images of themselves holding your books to help promote them. Check with each one first, but they should have no problem with you sharing their photo anywhere on social media.

7. You can build a separate story board for each of your books, adding images to represent what your characters look like, their homes, etc. to create imagery for settings or plots. You can also add images for your book teasers here to share.

8. One great way to expand your Pinterest audience/following is to link it to your Twitter or Facebook account so that any time you pin/share something there, it automatically shares on your other social media accounts as well. It's a good idea to include hashtags in your image captions when doing this. It really helps!

9. Not only is Pinterest good for "bookmarking" certain images/articles you like, it's a great way to find other like-minded people. Perfect strangers will follow you simply based on your likes (pins). It's a cool thing.

If you haven't tried Pinterest yet to market your books, you may want to reconsider. It can be a fun, unique tool if used correctly and respectfully (regarding intellectual property).

I will add that this site is more about networking with like-minded people than marketing your books, but that's the best way to reach your followers: becoming friends first.

Here is my Pinterest page. Feel free to follow me and connect! https://www.pinterest.com/tsanders2014/

TIP 279: Hashing out #hashtags

Twitter is an excellent resource in which to connect authors with fellow authors, and booklovers. However, it has its own set of unspoken rules that all Twitter friends should *follow* (pun totally intended). Some authors prefer Facebook, but I personally spend more time on Twitter. Mainly because, I don't have much time to be online during the day, and not much drama can fit into 140 characters. So, I've learned to make my Twitter time count.

Since Twitter posts only allow 140 characters, authors must make sure their posts are short and engaging. And, it's not recommended to use the maximum number of characters.

Here are some other ways to maximize your Twitter time:

- Don't use links in all your posts. It makes you appear sales-focused rather than social-networking focused.

- Tweet between 10-12 times per day. For these posts, a formula like this works well:
  5-6 informational or networking posts – no sales pitches – use links, images, and hashtags (perhaps links to other helpful blog posts, links to other authors' books, or just a nice image with a helpful writing tip.)

  2 just-for-fun posts – no links – just images or hashtags (I've included some samples below)

  2-3 sales posts – use links, images, and hashtags.

- When someone follows you, and you follow them back, go to their Twitter feed and try to retweet at least two of their interesting posts right away.

- You don't have to follow everyone who follows you, but you can retweet their tweets when they first follow you, if you want.

- If you choose not to follow someone back, you can send a quick "Thanks for following" message to acknowledge their effort.

- Offer funny, inspirational, intriguing, or thoughtful tweets. Images help a lot, too.

Before I share a list of helpful hashtags, let me just clarify what a hashtag really represents. Think of these little pound signs as clubs. Behind each hashtag exists a group of people who are interested in the hashtag topic. These people gather in the hashtag clubs and talk about that topic, follow links about that topic, and buy products that are associated with that topic. The trick is to make sure we (authors) offer what they are looking for in each of these hashtag clubs.

Here are some helpful hashtags to get you started:

#amwriting
#amreading
#mustread
#amediting
#bookworms
#booklovers
#authors
#indieauthors
#whattoread
#writerslife
#writingtips
#writerproblems
#authorproblems
#whattowrite
#books
#ebooks

#kindlebooks
#bookdeals
#99cents
#romance
#paranormal
#thriller
#suspense
#horror
#childrensbooks
#parenting
#selfhelp
#motivational
#humor
#womensfiction
#booksuggestions
#addictedtoreading

Hashtags are the bare bones of using Twitter, effectively.

TIP 280: Make a list and tweet it twice.
(more tips on Twitter)

I'm going to share with you how to build a strong Twitter following and KEEP your followers!

Don't be like the large utility companies that treat their new customers better than their existing ones. It's a quick way to lose followers and/or support for your cause (books, products, etc.)

Social media can be an overwhelming, time-consuming chasm if you don't manage it well. I'm not talking about using automated services here because I don't use them; therefore, I don't feel qualified enough to offer any advice about them.

I'm talking about making lists on Twitter. It's quite easy to do.

Here are the steps:

1. From your Twitter profile click on "Lists".

2. Click on "Create a New List" on the right-hand side of the page.

3. Title your list and choose whether you'd like it to be public or private and click "Save List".

4. A window will pop up for you to enter Twitter handles of persons you'd like to add to this particular list. Add away!

That's all there is to it. You are basically creating a "file" to be able to pull out any time you go to Twitter so you can tweet your most loyal "clients" (networking friends) first. If you are good to them, they will share your tweets as well. Don't depend on your new Twitter connections to do that for you.

Now when you visit your Twitter profile page, simply click on "Lists" again and it will pull up any lists you have created. Click on the name of a list and it will open the Twitter feed ONLY for that list. So, if you have twenty top friends on there, it will be much easier to sift through to be able to tweet their material first.

TIP 281: Addressing readers' concerns and questions

As I mentioned in a previous tip, authors should create a call to action at the end of each book they write. Something that encourages readers who've just read the book to take some kind of action that supports the author further and keeps the connection going. This could be in the form of leaving a review on Amazon or Goodreads, purchasing another book by that author, or contacting the author with any questions.

When or if the author receives questions or concerns about his or her book, those issues can be addressed in a number of ways.

- The author can post a blanket Q & A on his or her blog.

- A simple reply email can be sent out.

- The author can respond to the author on social media or Amazon via the review.

The type of response delivered depends on how/where the question was received and the author's preferred method of communication.

One way that has become quite popular recently in communicating with readers/fans and addressing issues about books is a podcast (basically a video).

Podcasts can be quite effective in connecting with readers/fans because it's a proven fact that humans identify with faces. And voices add personality to the faces in videos. So, when readers see and hear their favorite authors on a video, a human connection is formed. Instead of considering the author to be this untouchable, unreachable, unemotional entity upon whom he/she can unload every thought or opinion, the author is thought of as a person with feelings. Even I have changed my pre-formed opinions of certain authors once I met them in person or connected in a direct way (via the phone or video chat), or even in a non-direct way, such as watching a video of them.

In conclusion, when a reader has a question or concern about one of your books, consider creating a podcast to address it. Then post the podcast on your blog or website and/or tag the reader on social media so he/she can see that not only did you take his or her concern seriously, but you also took the time to offer a personal response.

You may grow a larger, loyal fan base with this one simple action.

TIP 282: Taking over Facebook (all about takeovers)

One way to reach new potential fans is by setting up a Facebook takeover party.

Think of a takeover as a party where YOU have the mic the entire time to capture the attention of all your guests. Usually these parties are scheduled in blocks of 30 minutes or 1 hour.

Here is how it works:

1. A Facebook friend (usually a fellow author or avid reader) sets aside a special day for the party and invites you to be a guest.

2. You choose a time frame to be able to post about your work.

3. Once your time frame is set, you start preparing your materials and inviting your friends to the party.

4. Materials you need to have at the ready include: cover images of your books to share, teasers (if available), buy links for your books as well as any other links for your trailers, short excerpts (literally no more than maybe two paragraphs) of your book, an author photo to share (candid ones are best for this type of party), and maybe a few funny or engaging memes as well.

5. Depending on your allotted time frame, you will be posting once per 5-6 minutes for either party you choose. Therefore, you will need to have about 6 posts at the ready for a 30-minute party and 9 or 10 posts for a 1-hour party.

6. If you plan to offer giveaway items, you need to make sure to have them in hand (or available once the party ends) to gift to the winners. Most authors offer at least one free digital copy of each of their books and/or a gift card of some sort.

7. Now that you know the day, time, duration, and necessary materials for your takeover, you will need to know what type of posts to have ready.

8. POST 1: Introduce yourself, tell what genre you write, where you are from, and offer a bit of personal information about yourself. It's also nice to ask where all the guests are from. They seem to enjoy that.

9. POST 2: Get right to the fun stuff; that's why the guests are there. Tell what you are giving away during your party. Most authors offer at least one digital copy of their books and/or a gift card of some sort. Tell the guests what they need to do to enter the contest. Also, be sure to state: Facebook is not affiliated with this giveaway—official Facebook thing one must say.

10. POST 3 and 4 are fillers – include book trailers, teaser images, and funny or inspirational memes. You can offer chances to enter your contest by guests doing any of these things:

   • Following one of your social media pages

   • "LIKING" one of your book trailers on YouTube

   • Subscribing to your blog
   (Ask them to come back to the takeover site and type "done" or "got you" or something like that to confirm they did these things.)

11. POST 5: Introduce your second book (or if you only have one, continue with memes or teasers). Tell guests what to

do to enter the contest to win a free copy of this book. Some ideas are:

- Pay it forward and ask them to "LIKE" a fellow author's social media page or book-trailer page.

- Ask them to describe their most romantic date (if for a romance book), perhaps their scariest moment (for horror), their favorite quote from a book (for general). People love to talk about themselves.

12. POST 6: This is probably your last post, if you have a 30-minute party. Be sure to thank all the guests, remind them where/how to find you, share your books' buy links and blog links, and tell them when the party ends and how you will be choosing the winners. Be sure to thank the host and guests once more before you sign off.

If you have an hour-long party, you can fill time by offering more memes, teasers, links for your book trailers, talking about your blog, anything to push YOU.

There you have it—everything you need to have a successful Facebook takeover party. Be sure to promptly choose your winners when you say you will and deliver the gifts to them. It's always fun for them to have their names announced on Facebook by tagging, or you can post it in a discussion feed on the takeover party page, or on your own blog. That's what I do.

TIP 283: Live readings ... to build your fan base

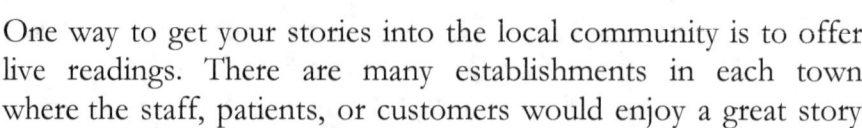

One way to get your stories into the local community is to offer live readings. There are many establishments in each town where the staff, patients, or customers would enjoy a great story while they wait for something.

However, you must consider your target audience. For instance, you probably wouldn't want to go read a horror book excerpt to a group of people in a nursing home.

Also, you don't have to be the one reading your book. You are welcome to hire someone or have a friend who speaks eloquently to read your story while you manage the signing and selling of your books. It's always a great idea, if the venue permits, to do a live reading of an excerpt at your book signing events.

Here are fifteen places you might try to set up a live reading of your book:

1. Library – typically they offer live readings once per week, in a private room.

2. Hospital – children's books for children's hospitals, adult books for regular hospitals. Most of the long-term patients will simply enjoy the company.

3. A retirement community – maybe a lodge or golf club, bridge club, bingo club – these folks have nothing but time, usually.

4. A school – depending on the level of children's books you offer. Middle-grade fiction works for middle-school aged

children. Picture books work well with Kindergarten through second or third grade.

5. A local book store.

6. Online – via YouTube or other social media platforms (Facebook, Goodreads, etc.) – post a video clip reading of your book.

7. Local colleges – for YA or adult – perhaps an English class

8. A military base or military (spousal) support groups

9. A local girl scouts or boy scouts group – especially for early reader books and chapter books

10. Local book clubs – physical book clubs.

11. A local girl scouts or boy scouts group – especially for early reader books and chapter books.

12. A local church – especially if your book is faith-based or is a children's book you could read during children's church or Sunday school

13. Local fire houses or police stations – especially for crime thrillers or mysteries

14. Children's books or parenting guides – local mom/baby store

15. Local art studio or music store

Live readings are a great way to expand your fan base and build your confidence as a writer and speaker.

TIP 284: Online groups for authors

The writing journey can be a lonely one. Many friends and family members start avoiding us, afraid we might ask them—yet again—to review our books or even read our books, or that we might talk about our books. We often notice our "shares and likes" from these people, dwindling down little by little on social media, even though they used to comment on our every post (BA – before authorhood) that is. It happens.

That's why it's important to find people who are supportive. Authors need like-minded friends to bounce ideas off of, to read and critique their work, to network with, and simply to share their woes and achievements in the process. Sometimes, our friends and family don't even want to hear about our exciting accomplishments, especially if they haven't achieved something in life they'd hope to as well. It's human nature (for some).

Thankfully, there are people (besides our readers) who DO want to talk about our books and all things related to the writing process. You just have to know where to look for these people.

Today I am sharing a bit of information about some groups I belong to on social media, groups of people I recommend. I call these people "my tribe."

Every author needs a tribe.

Books Go Social – this online group has two separate platforms – one for authors and one for readers. Both are on Twitter and Facebook.

Books Go Social – Author's Group – Facebook
I've been a member of this group for a few years now and have met some amazing people who have become close friends and

beta readers. They offer support on Twitter and Facebook by way of Likes, Shares, Retweets, as well as reading/reviewing my books.

Here are some details about BGS:

- membership is FREE

- the club has over 10,000 members (and growing) to network with, get writing tips from, and just run things by.

- with such a large member base, I have met editors, graphic designers, book trailer makers, etc. You may just find the right person to help you with a publishing/designing issue.

- members purchase/review one another's books and post them on Amazon, Goodreads, and BGS Reader's Group on FB

Books Go Social – Readers Group – Facebook

This group is Facebook based. They do tweet sometimes, but not as much as connecting on Facebook. The cool thing about this group is that it is strictly about BOOKS! The only self-promotion allowed is based on the author's first name. He/she is only allowed to promote on the day of the month that corresponds with his/her first name. (Ex: My name starts with a "T" and I promote on the 20th of each month.) It really helps with the spamming.

Here is what you will find in this group:

- it's also FREE to join

- it is comprised of readers who talk about books they have read and recommend to like-minded members

- members (authors and readers) can post a review for another member's book they've read – or they can suggest another member's book

- readers can find their next "great read" in this area and repost about it on their timeline or a friend's timeline. They can also tweet about it or share it on other social sites.

So, Books Go Social has two great options to choose from. They also have paid promotional packages if you need more marketing help. Be sure to check them out at booksgosocial.com.

Readers Review Room:

This is a Facebook group I created for readers and authors to connect in a no-pressure environment. You won't find self-indulgent promos here, but you also won't find writing tips or critique groups. Only three people have permission to post in this group, and we only post promos for books that are listed on our site, and reviews submitted by our reviewers for these books.

I do share occasional information about writing contests and other author resources, but there are only four to five posts per day total in this group. It's not saturated.

This is a public group, and all members are allowed to comment; however, I moderate all comments. There is NO author bashing or harassment in this group!

So, if you seek a place to find great (honest) book recommendations, and network with other bookish type of people, please join us!
https://www.facebook.com/groups/readersreviewroom/

And last but not least, one of my favorite writers' groups – Writers and Authors … and Readers.

The people in this group are extremely nice, respectful, encouraging, and helpful.

It's highly moderated, so no foul language or non-family-oriented posts are allowed. Also, self-promotion is only allowed on certain days of the week.

To learn more about this group, visit this link:

https://www.facebook.com/groups/writersandauthorsforum/

TIP 285: Social media etiquette

Authors know how to use words like weapons for evil, or tools for good, depending on the situation. We know that with the right words, we can make a person feel like the lowest scum of the earth or an angel who just earned wings. That's *our* superpower. But as it goes with all superheroes, with great power comes great responsibility.

Just because we know what to say and how to say it, doesn't mean we *should* say it, especially on social media.

Earlier in these tips, I mentioned that some authors use their books to vent and rant about personal conflicts or opinions, which, unless it's done delicately and professionally, is not a good idea.

The same rings true for social media accounts.

Even if using a pen name (screen name) many authors tend to form personal relationships with some of their fans and begin to feel a sense of comfort in being able to say *anything* to these people, concerning *any subject*. But this is not always a wise decision. **Just because an author and a fan agree on a few things, does not mean that they will agree on every topic, especially sensitive ones like politics, religion, and even familial issues such as child rearing.**

It's wise to remember that anything you say on social media can (and often *will*) be used against you, not always in a court of law, but many times in a much harsher court—society in general. People can be downright hateful if they feel their personal values and opinions are being attacked—even by the simplest comment. Again, tone cannot be detected over text alone, so that person may not realize you are joking, or if you are trying to be neutral on a topic.

All it takes is ONE comment or post to taint (and even ruin) an author's credibility online. And you never know who is reading your comments!

So, if you feel the need to bash a certain fellow author, or a reader who left a bad review, or a social media group or company, just remember, the Internet has eyes everywhere, and the Internet is forever!

This goes for all social media interactions, from a drawn-out rant in a blog post to a snappy Twitter post you think no one is reading, and you simply *must* get something off your chest.

Proper social media etiquette is so much more than just refraining from blasting others with thoughtless comments.

Here are a few more Do's and Don'ts concerning social media etiquette. Most of these apply to professional (author) pages; but remember, things on the Internet are always interconnected, "inter" being the key word here.

1. Do take the time to use proper grammar and punctuation, especially if you are an author. Readers pay attention to these things and silently, or sometimes publicly, critique you.

2. Don't post embarrassing pictures of yourself on your timeline or feed—pictures of you drunk at a party, pictures of you right after having dental surgery (with drool dripping down your chin), pictures of you in a bikini or showing too much skin. These types of things are best shared in private messages, because, especially on Facebook, people love to see other people at their worst. It makes them feel good about themselves. So, don't post something that you wouldn't want the whole world to see. Keep a professional image. Professionals don't have the

luxury of posting anything they want, and even though I try not to be judgmental, I even sometimes think a little less of people (who claim to be professionals) posting pictures of this nature. Being human and candid is one thing, but disrespecting yourself and your reputation is a whole other issue.

3. Don't join an abundance of social media groups if you don't have time to interact. All that does is fill up your feed, not allowing you much of a chance to see the posts of those you truly wish to support.

4. Don't put personal contact information on public posts—personal email addresses, phone numbers, physical addresses. I see this all the time, when two people think they are having a private conversation. It's just so dangerous!

5. Don't add your "friends" to social media groups without their permission. This fills up their feeds and usually ticks them off.

6. Don't tag your "friends" in an abundance of giveaways, contests, or posts. That can be annoying as well.

7. Of course, don't give out your "friends'" personal contact information to anyone else without permission.

8. Don't constantly post about every aspect of your day/life. I see people posting every single time they go to the gym, or every dinner they eat, or every outfit their kid wears to school. Just … don't.

9. Do share interesting (neutral) articles and posts with people who might find them helpful. It may be best (for controversial topics especially) to head the post with something like: "This is not my personal opinion; I just found it interesting. What do you all think?".

10. Do share pictures of yourself at book signings and events, with fans, and at conferences—and receiving any honors that have to do with your profession.

11. Do (it's okay to) share personal pics of your family, if you are okay with the content, and your friends are okay with you sharing. This shows your personal/human side and shouldn't be done all the time, but on occasion.

12. Do support friends and acquaintances on social media, especially if they support you. Don't make it all about you every time. Congratulate them on their promotion. Tell them you hope they feel well soon when they are sick. Send words of encouragement when they are going through something stressful or sad.

13. Don't believe or trust everything you see on social media. I can't tell you how many times I've spoken to my friends, in person, after seeing their "beautiful" family pics on Facebook, and mentioned that I'm so happy for them or I've congratulated them on having such a nice life ... only for them to say to me, "Don't believe everything you see on Facebook. My life sucks." Nearly everyone I speak to about things like this tells me, "Facebook is a mask. It's not really how life is for most people." And I think that's sad but true.

These are just a few ways to interact with integrity on social media. You can be human and still be kind, considerate ... and private. Just because it happens to you, doesn't mean everyone should know about it—or *wants* to know about it, for that matter.

TIP 286: Engage your Twitter audience with a Q & A session

Here's a quick tip to help you engage on Twitter and gain more followers. It's somewhat of a Twitter game but it's also an efficient way to network with like-minded people.

Host a Q and A session on Twitter.

It doesn't have to be set up like a formal interview. In fact, the more casual it appears, the less pressure Twitter friends will feel in "playing the game."

Basically, you are "fishing" for information on your followers to find your target audience.

Here are some example "fishing" questions.
Using the words "And GO!" after your question tends to liven up the post and engage more people.

1. What are you reading at the moment?

2. What's your favorite line so far in the book you're currently reading?

3. What's your favorite genre to read?

4. What's the title of the last book you read?

5. What's the title of the book that's up next on your Kindle TBR list?

You can also "fish" to gain insight on what readers look for in a novel in your writing genre:

1. What's your least favorite thing about a main male/female character?

2. Name one thing that ruins a romance novel for you.

3. Romance novels – sappy or sexy? Which do you prefer?

4. What's the first thing you look for when choosing a new book?

5. Which matters more – book cover or blurb?

6. What's one thing that makes you one-click an e-book?

These are just a few questions you can throw out into your Twitter feed (or Facebook timeline) to gain insight on your followers or to narrow down your target audience. This game will let you know who is engaged in your feed, but it will also give you an idea of how and where to market your books.

TIP 287: Networking with local authors to build your fan base

One way to build your brand in your area is to network with local authors. You can find them on social media quite often.

On Facebook, you may see a group called "Texas Writers and Readers" or something like that. Or you can do a general search for "writers" or "readers" groups and then ask who lives near you.

You can also Google book clubs (physical book clubs) in your area and connect with local readers and/or writers.

The saying "there is power in numbers" is true. You may find local authors who are willing to do a multi-genre showcase or event with you. Perhaps at a local craft fair or an event hall that you rent. If several authors are participating, the cost could be significantly less.

The lesser cost isn't the only benefit to doing a multi-genre event. Having more options for a wider variety of readers will draw more attention to your table or booth. (something for everyone)

Don't look at authors, even those who write in your same genre, as your competition. View them as allies in winning the war against the bad reputation Indie authors often receive.

But there are a few things to keep in mind:

1. Make sure you check out the other authors' books on Amazon to ensure they align with the quality of yours. You wouldn't want to be a Christian author who ends up having an erotic romance author show up with suggestive

banners or book covers at a local church event you orchestrated.

2. Make sure you all agree on splitting the cost of the event – table, venue rental, and even decor.

3. Make sure you don't overbook your table to the point that some books wouldn't even be seen.

4. Make sure you all take part in cleaning the place up when your event is over, to leave a good impression on the leasing representative, for future events.

5. Try to talk with this person over the phone at least once to get a feel of his or her personality. Is she a Negative Nelly? Is he a Boisterous Bob? Does she run off at the mouth, dropping the f-bomb every few minutes? Does he tell racial jokes or demean women? These are not deal breakers for everyone, but like I said, make sure the people you choose to participate in your event, represent your standards, as they will be interacting with the same potential customers you do. Not to mention, you will be forced to sit beside these people for possibly several hours! Everyone needs to be professional.

Connecting with authors in your home town or nearby towns can be the beginning of beautiful friendships, critique groups, support systems, and hopefully increased sales – if it's done right.

TIP 288: Making the most of Goodreads

I'm a member of Goodreads (a.k.a. GR), although, I don't use it as often as other social media platforms like Facebook and Twitter. There is a great deal to learn about it, but if you take the time to do so, you can build a strong following as an author.

I have limited knowledge of this huge arena for authors, but I'll share what I know.

Essentially, Goodreads is the Facebook for authors and readers.

Here are a few perks of using Goodreads to promote yourself:

- The entire membership is filled with book lovers!

- Authors and readers can join targeted discussion groups, per genre or theme.

- It's a great place to network with other authors.

- Authors can sync their blogs to their Goodreads profile to save time in sharing posts.

- Authors can offer pre-release or new-release giveaways.

- Reviews posted on Goodreads are automatically generated on several other sites, helping authors gain exposure.

- Authors can discover new favorite authors (as readers), while building their fan base.

- It's a great place to announce book events – online or in-person, because the membership is massive and target-rich.

- Authors are in charge of their own profiles, with the ability to add anything they wish – videos, quizzes, widgets, etc.,

Here are a few things authors can do to make the most of Goodreads:

1. Add a bio and a nice picture. It doesn't have to be your face, but studies have proven that people connect with faces.

2. Add a few books to your "shelf" (basically, your TBR list), and share your list with others.

3. Search for like-minded readers and authors – socialize. Send them friend requests. Generally, people are quite friendly on GR.

4. Connect your blog to GR.

5. Post videos, excerpts, etc., to draw readers to your page.

6. Don't join a ton of groups, unless you plan to interact. The members of those groups can get quite testy about drifters (those who drift in and out of groups just long enough to promote themselves).

7. Readers and authors enjoy quizzes. Create one and share it.

8. Add the GR widget to your blog/site to promote your GR reviews.

As far as GR giveaways, here are five tips, straight from GR, to maximize your results:

https://www.goodreads.com/blog/show/607-five-tips-for-running-a-giveaway-on-goodreads

I think of Goodreads as a huge library that hosts individual book clubs. Some groups can be cliquey, but once you find a few groups that house members you enjoy networking with, Goodreads can be a great place to hang out with other book-minded folks, or, as I call them (us), book nerds.

TIP 289: Ten ways authors can strengthen the Indie industry

As a mom, I've reprimanded my children several times for "making me (our family) look bad" through inappropriate behavior, or even through inappropriate attire for a certain occasion. It's my job to make sure my children understand how to dress and behave properly to reflect our (mine and my husband's) standards as a family unit.

The Indie publishing industry is a family—of sorts—as well. Each author must do his or her part to strengthen the industry and uphold its reputation of excellence. In other words, we must each do our part to "make our family look good."

Here are ten ways to help strengthen the Indie publishing industry:

1. Support your fellow Indie authors. I don't mean you have to buy and read only Indie books, but do try to share their promos and events, and add a few of their books to your TBR list in addition to your classic favorites. Supporting the Indie industry is like supporting a small business. There are some amazingly talented Indie authors whose books are every bit as polished and professional as traditionally published ones.

2. Make sure your book is professionally edited.

3. Make sure you have a professional book cover and formatting.

4. Don't steal copyrighted material from other authors.

5. Don't promote idle gossip about other authors or retaliate against fellow authors with low reviews.

6. Don't be a hypocrite. When you see a favorite music artist's songs on free download (pirated copies), don't download them. Buy them and support those artists, just as you would want to be supported in real book sales. These artists are people just like you.

7. Share other Indie authors' books with your friends and family when they ask for book recommendations.

8. Offer great writing. Go through the channels it takes to produce great books: writing, revising, rewriting, and editing, before publishing.

9. Don't spam timelines and targeted groups. This puts a bad taste in readers' mouths about Indie authors, because, I assure you, their favorite traditionally published authors DON'T spam them.

10. Wear your Indie title proudly. Don't let anyone convince you or label you as being "too lazy to get a real publishing deal," or "not good enough to get a real publishing deal."

Indie authors must have these things in place to succeed in the publishing industry:

1. Knowledge of the publishing process.

2. Great writing skills—knowledge of grammar and writing mechanics.

3. A tough skin to combat all the negativity.

4. A solid marketing plan.

5. A personal support system, and a professional one (editors, cover designers, etc.,).

These things help produce quality books, which strengthen the industry and keep our family *looking good*.

And remember, we Indie authors are not in competition with one another. We are competing against the stigma that surrounds the Indie publishing industry!

Two of my blog followers added these thoughts:

To these I add, no troll-like behavior, even if you think it's just mild. Occasionally I find myself appalled at what indie authors post or say about others, or how they talk to others. Thanks, Traci.
Stephen Geez

I think you've covered everything here, Traci. All good advice. The only thing I would add is, never give up. It doesn't matter how long it takes to get your story done right, keep working at it. You are under no deadline but the one you set for yourself, if any. I don't set deadlines. I work better that way after a lifetime of deadlines to meet before I retired from the clerical world. You're the boss. Let's make the Indie industry sparkle.
Sharon K. Connell

TIP 290: Ten ways to "pay it forward" as an author

I'm all about paying it forward, in my career and my life in general. I never regret helping another person because, even if that person doesn't seem to appreciate my gesture, that doesn't mean it wasn't needed. Some people have a hard time accepting help or kind gestures. Perhaps it makes them feel weak, or obligated to return the favor.

But this is not what the spirit of giving is supposed to be about.

Paying it forward basically involves you doing something nice for another person, in return for a different person having done something nice for you.

For instance, my friend once posted on Facebook that a person in front of her in line at Starbucks paid for her coffee. My friend, in turn, paid for the person behind her.

Now, the process doesn't always keep going like that. As I said before, some people will resist gestures like these, reasoning that they don't take handouts, or something to that effect. Others will be grateful and will gladly pay it forward.

The same types of situations may occur in our careers as authors. I've had many people help me in my writing/publishing career, and I'm happy to help others in any way I can. Some people try to return the favor, but I never expect it.

You don't always have to buy a fellow author's book to support him or her, especially if you don't read that genre.

One thing I do is gift copies of other authors' books to winners in giveaways, rather than my own books. Not every time, of course, but quite often. I don't even tell the author about it most of the time. If he/she is part of the takeover or launch party, of course my gift will be revealed, but sometimes I participate in takeovers and gift random authors' books. It's fun, and the winners are almost always taken aback by my generosity. But that's not why I do it.

Here are ten other ways to pay it forward to your fellow authors:

1. When you join a group on Facebook or Goodreads, don't always promote your own books. Mention your fellow authors' books, on occasion.

2. Tweet about another author's books.

3. Create promo teasers for another author's books, and share them on various social media platforms.

4. Offer to interview a fellow author on your blog. I'm always thrilled when fellow bloggers invite me to guest post.

5. If you know avid readers who enjoy certain genres your author friends write in, mention your friends' books to those people; or at the least, share a link on social media. The friend will be happy that you know him or her so well, and the author might get a new sale, and a new fan.

6. If you hear about book events, new agents who seek certain genres, or writing contests you think certain author friends of yours might do well in, send them the links or information.

7. Offer video book reviews for your favorite authors' books.

8. Send a fellow author an e-card (tons of sites offer free e-cards now) just to say *hi* or *thanks*. You never know who needs a smile that day. Many of my author friends do this

for me, and those cards always seem to come right when I need them.

9. Share new releases or special sales of your fellow authors' books on your social media pages to help them get the word out.

10. Comment on a fellow author's blog posts, instead of simply reading them.

These are just a few ways to support your fellow authors. We are not put on this earth to focus on our own health and success all the time. We're here to make the world a better place. And we do this by being better people. Giving when we don't have it. Returning a favor, even if the original giver won't accept it. We find a way to help better another person's life, even with the smallest of gestures.

As the old proverb goes: "When your hand is open to give, it is also open to receive."

And remember, blessings are not always the ones we pray for. Sometimes they're the ones we didn't even know we wanted or needed.

TIP 291: Oops! Your human side is showing. (connecting with fans personally)

This tip is all about getting personal with your readers.

As an avid reader and author, I must admit, I get a bit star-struck when my favorite authors connect with me on a personal level. It makes me feel special, and I'm thankful that I've been able to experience that feeling.

Now, when I write something a reader enjoys, I know how important it is to thank that reader for taking the time to not only read and review my book, but to also reach out to me on a personal level. It's an astounding feeling.

So, my point is, even though I can completely identify with the need to keep your personal life private, the readers need to get to know you. They want to see pictures of you to place a face with a name. They want to hear your voice to place a personality with a face. Reach out to them as much as possible, and share a little bit of the real you.

I feel it's important for my readers to connect with me on a personal level, to get to know who I am as a person, a mom, and a wife—not just an author—especially since I write nonfiction parenting books. My experiences in these roles help establish authenticity in my writing.

In this spirit, I've shared some personal photos on my blog, if you'd like to know more about me.

http://awordwithtraci.com/tip-31-oops-your-human-side-is-showing-connecting-personally-with-fans/

TIP 292: Expanding your audience by guest blogging

Over the past few months, I've had several bloggers contact me to let me know they enjoyed an article I wrote, and they wanted to know if I would link to a similar article on their blog, or if I would allow them to offer guest posts on my blog.

I realized this could be a cool endeavor for me, with the right people.

Just as I offered other posts in this segment about networking with local authors and authors online, it's also a good idea to network with other bloggers, and even collaborate with some if your values align. This isn't about contacting bloggers for book tours. This is about sharing content.

Working with other bloggers can expose your writing and ideas to their audiences, and the more bloggers you build trustworthy relationships with, the larger your following becomes.

As I've mentioned before, you never know who other people know!

Here are a few things to keep in mind when contacting other bloggers:

1. Make sure you are not insulting this person by offering content that is too similar to theirs, or that may seem like copycat versions of theirs. (The people who contact me simply expand on my topics, or have interesting twists to my topics. I don't mind entertaining their ideas because I know that two heads can be better than one.)

2. Make sure to research the person's blog to learn more about him/her. Does this person's values and ideas align

with yours? Are there any offending posts on there that you might be associated with – political, religious, or even gender-based?

3. Make sure to read through any material that is sent to you, thoroughly checking for grammatical errors and sensitive content that you might not want to be associated with. Let the blogger know if you see something you don't agree with.

4. Be courteous in your guest posts. Thank the host for allowing you to post there, and be sure to reciprocate on your blog – perhaps share an article of theirs that you enjoyed, or review a book written by the blogger, if he/she is an author.

5. Don't make your blog posts too long or monotonous. Remember, the blogger has to read it to vet it for his/her site, and the blogger's visitors have to read it as well. Make sure the post is just as you would represent it on your own blog.

6. Help send more traffic to the blogger's site by promoting your post (with the blogger's link) on your social ,media pages. Win-win for both.

These are just a few ways to network with fellow bloggers. If you build solid friendships with certain bloggers and you happen to run across an article or some tips that might coincide with what he/she blogs about, be a friend and pass it on. Readers don't care where the content comes from as long as it's great content.

The blogger will thank you.

I can speak from experience on this because I have blogger friends who send links and topics to me constantly. Some I use, some I don't, but I always appreciate them thinking of me.

TIP 293: Re-purposing and re-blogging content to build your following

For those of you who run into situations where you can't think of anything to blog about, there is hope. Many bloggers re-purpose their own material or re-blog material from other sites and blogs.

If a certain news topic is circling the Internet or television, and you previously published a compatible article on your blog, you can gain some *new* viewers for your writing (and your blog in general) by re-posting that article. As long as the content is relevant and helpful, people will be interested in reading it, to keep in line with current trends.

As well, if you happen upon a blog post that offers answers about a certain topic circling the writing community, you could become known as the go-to person for "discovering" helpful articles on important writing topics.

The problem some bloggers face in doing this is not becoming known for their own unique ideas. Re-purposing your own material is one thing but only offering material from other bloggers is mostly shining a light on *their* writing, not yours.

I personally re-blog on rare occasion, and only if I find something that might be useful for others.

Re-blogging borders on plagiarism if not done correctly, so one must be careful and follow some simple etiquette guidelines.

1. Always get permission to re-blog the material. Most times, a simple "re-blog" or share button of some sort will appear at the end of the article.

2. Be sure to ask the blogger what method of sharing he/she prefers. Again, the share buttons may clarify this.

3. Always give full credit to the blogger who provided the content. I personally offer links only, with my own thoughts as an introduction.

4. Most times the blogger will ask that you only share the first few paragraphs of a post and include a link back to the original site if his or her content is used.

5. Sometimes the original author of the content will have comments/likes features turned off because he/she may not be able to interact with those commenters.

6. If you do re-blog content, be sure to introduce the original author and add your own thoughts on why you are sharing the content.

7. Don't fill your feed up with re-blogged material. It makes you appear to not have original thoughts.

8. Make sure you read the entire post before sharing. There could be something of a sensitive nature within that you may not want to convey to your own audience.

Most of all, respect each individual blogger's procedures for sharing. When in doubt, it never hurts to ask how he/she would prefer the material to be distributed. Most bloggers are happy to share their work as long as they are credited properly.

Just in case you're wondering, I don't mind anything of mine being shared/re-blogged. I can't control where it goes or what people do with it, and I won't stress myself out trying to do so. Plus, I know that I always have the original work in my files, so I can prove/disprove whatever arises in conflict.

After you Publish Part 3 Building Your Brand Through Blogging

TIP 294: Do I really need a blog/site?

Many authors, especially those new to publishing wonder: *Do I need to blog?*

Many other questions arise when authors start marketing their books. Do I need a social media account? Do I need an email list? Do I need to schedule book signings?

This tip will focus on blogging.

While no online presence is required for any author to be successful, it is helpful in connecting with existing fans, and it's an inexpensive platform where authors can present their work to the public.

Blogging can aide an author's career in several ways:

1. It provides a platform for an author to express his or her views on a variety of topics. Only so many subjects can be discussed in radio and magazine interviews.

2. It provides a platform for an author to present all of his or her titles. During interviews, authors usually only have time to discuss a few select books.

3. It provides a platform for readers/fans to learn more about and connect with their favorite authors, on their own schedule, rather than having to arrange attendance for in-person events. Some fans have no clue what their favorite authors look like.

4. It provides a platform for authors to share all their writing, even those unpublished. It also allows an author a place to

hone his or her writing skills through blog posts and articles, short stories, etc.

5. It provides a central place where agents and publishers can go to learn more about authors and contact them easily, and see what type of following the author has.

6. Finally, a blog can serve as a platform for an author to network with other authors, supporting them through posts and blog tours. Networking is a great way for authors to expand their audience.

In summation, does an author *need* a blog? No. But it does help authors expand their following and showcase their writing skills in general, rather than focusing on just one writing piece at a time.

TIP 295: Website or blog?

Did you know there is a difference between a website and a blog? Websites tend to be more static, whereas blogs lean more toward interaction with visitors.

But which one is right for your business/brand? It all depends on what you wish to accomplish.

Here are a few details about websites vs. blogs:

Website:

1. It's generally a static page and isn't updated as frequently as a blog.

2. It does not typically allow (encourage) interaction with (or comments from) visitors.

3. It usually centers around a certain theme or brand, and doesn't change often.

4. It tends to rank higher in search engines for more consistent periods of time.

5. Typically, websites have more content to keep visitors on the page longer.

Blog:

1. Its content can change frequently in theme.

2. It is typically updated daily, weekly, or monthly.

3. Its content is typically subjective—based on personal opinions and current trends.

4. Allows interaction with (and comments from) visitors.

5. Doesn't typically sell a brand or product, but a "person or idea" instead.

6. Ranking in search engines can skyrocket or plummet quickly, depending on content.

7. Visitors tend to only read the "most current" post and then move on, rather than look around or hang around the page.

8. Blogs tend to get hacked more often than websites because they are more relaxed with security options.

Now that you know a little bit more about each type of online platform, answer these questions to decide which one is right for you:

1. Do you want to allow interaction with your visitors? – if so, blog is better.

2. Do you want to allow visitors to comment on your page? – if so, blog is better.

3. Are you selling a product or simply trying to network? if so, website is better.

4. Do you have time to devote to updating content often? – not much? – website is better.

5. How much do you want to spend in setup and ongoing maintenance? – not much or none – blog is better (websites can be expensive to set up and maintain).

6. Who is your target audience and what do you want to say to them? Ongoing events and news? – blog is better.

Ongoing (same-product or company) sales? — website is better.

As you can see, it all depends on what your goals are for creating a site or blog. I personally have created a site that operates more like a blog, and it works great for what I want to accomplish.

Either way, unless you are familiar with html code, back-end operations, and spyware programs, it's best to hire a professional to create either one of these, if you want a clean, virus-free site/page.

TIP 296: Creating your "about me" page

Some authors/bloggers offer great tips and topics but may find it difficult to write the "about me" page for their blogs or sites. One reason this may be is, some people feel awkward talking about themselves to others. Another reason could be that they don't know *how* to write something like this.

The interesting thing about the "about me" page is that it's not just all about you! It's also your chance to let your readers/audience know what you can do for *them*. What service do you provide? What types of posts will you offer? What is your level of interaction with your followers? What can you give them that they can't find anywhere else, or at least not as easily?

A few key items can make a huge difference in how an author is perceived by his/her target audience. As well, the length of the bio is an important element—not too long or too short.

Here are 7 things an author should include on the "about me" page:

1. **What you provide: a profile photo**

   A professional or, at the very least, pleasant author photo. No candid snapshots from your smartphone unless they are high res and decent-looking—not ones where you are drunk or in a bikini or something. You may still get followers, but probably not the type you are aiming for.

   What it does for your audience:

   This part of the post tells your readers what you look like so they can put a face with a name. It also allows them to learn a bit about your personality (by what you wear, if you smile or not, if you wear glasses, about what age you might be, if you have any identifiable marks (tattoos, abundant jewelry or makeup, etc.).

2. **What you provide: short bio**

   You don't have to list every single award or writing contest you've won, or every book you've written, if you have several in one genre. Provide a few titles or even just the genre(s) you write. Tell how long you've been writing and how you got started, to let readers know a little bit about your journey.

   A bio can read one of two ways: in third-person POV, as if an editor or publisher wrote it about you, or in first-person, if you write it about yourself. Either is acceptable. The formality of it all depends on your purpose and audience for the blog/site. If you are blogging simply to offer book reviews or interact with others on a casual level, then your "about me" page doesn't have to be so formal. But if you offer any type of professional advice and strive to present yourself as an authority in a subject or field, it's best to provide a few clean, concise paragraphs about your background, without getting too personal.

   What it does for your audience:

   This part of the page tells your readers why you are qualified to offer the types of posts that you do. What makes you the expert in your topics?

3. **What you provide: a bit of personal information (other than your writing credentials)**
   Include just a few other hobbies you have, besides writing, that may encourage others to connect with you: dancing, singing, cooking, yoga, etc.

What it does for your audience:

This part of the post lets your followers know they are connecting with a real person—one who has other interests besides blogging or writing in general. Believe it or not, those who follow blogs, read books, and write books have other interests they like to discuss on occasion.

4. **What you provide: contact links**
   Include contact links at the bottom of the page so that as soon as readers have learned a little bit about you and are still in the mindset to connect with you, they can go straight to your social media pages and follow.

   What it does for your audience:
   Contact links offer a way for your blog visitors to connect with you outside of the blog, just in case they want to learn more about you.

5. **What you provide: a call to action**

   Include a call-to-action type of link at the bottom of the page—one that is hyperlinked to at least one other page on your blog. Perhaps an article or a short piece of writing. The longer a visitor stays on your blog, the better your chances of gaining a new follower.

   What it does for your audience:

   A call to action does two things: gives your visitor something to do after reading your page, and it offers the visitor a chance to look around other places on your blog.

6. **What you provide: mission statement**

   You can mention your goal for the blog/site on your "about me" page if you want to duplicate the mission portion of your front page. If you don't have a mission statement on your blog, consider creating one and placing it on the front page. Otherwise, include it on the "about me" page.

What it does for your audience:

This part tells your visitors what they can expect if they stick around on your blog, or decide to subscribe.

Ultimately, the "about me" page serves as somewhat of a resume or application. The interviewer is the visitor to your blog—the who might become a loyal follower. You must show your human side while maintaining an appropriate level of professionalism. And just like an application or resume, your "about me" page can determine if a follower sticks around or if they move on to interview someone else.

Here is my "about me" page if you'd like to take a look: http://awordwithtraci.com/about/

TIP 297: Tips for successful blogging

I've been blogging for a few years and have done extensive research on this craft.

Blogging truly is a craft. It takes time to find your voice and niche, and even longer to see the results of your efforts.

I've connected with several talented bloggers, studied many blogs, and asked a great number of questions to come up with the tips I'm providing here. But we'll get to those in a moment.

Before you start blogging, and before you even get into the deeper aspects of blogging, there are a few things you need to ask yourself:

- Why do I want to blog? What message am I intending (hoping) to get out to the world?

- What main topic do I want to blog about?

- Do I have time to blog? Blogging takes a great deal of time to write the posts, edit them, and even search for the right pictures to accompany the posts.

- Do I have the personality to blog? Am I easily offended? (for when visitors leave comments on posts)

- Is there a need for what I wish to blog about?

These are just the basic questions to ask yourself before setting up your blog. Once you have determined that you do in fact have a valid reason to blog and are willing to put in the time and effort it requires, you can move on to these steps. We'll start at the beginning, assuming you have not set up a blog yet.

Here are some basic tips to get you started on your blogging journey:

1. Decide on your blog theme and domain name. It needs to be something easy to remember, easy to spell, and something that identifies with what you wish to accomplish with your blog. (Example: I once had a site for health and wellness titled *Taking Back My Temple*. It was a personal phrase and motivator for me because I was in a stage of life where I was ready to take back control of my body and my health. It also resonated with many others. But it wasn't what I was truly passionate about, so I didn't keep up with it.)

2. Decide on a logo and a slogan. Again, this needs to identify with your goals for the site and your personality. (Mine for this site happens to be: "You're in the *write* place," because everything on my blog is writing related in some way.)

3. Decide who your target audience is and where you will find them.

4. Decide what your first post will be about. What is the first thing you want your (potential) readers to know about you and your site? Make it intriguing, and unique, because it's your first impression on the world. And the Internet is forever!

Okay, now all the technical stuff is out of the way, it's time to blog.

Here are some tips for an eye-catching, engaging, memorable blog post:

1. Use various colors and styles of fonts to stress a point. (Ex: a certain word or phrase you'd like to stand out in the post. Try to do at least one line or phrase per one or two

paragraphs. I use colors in all my posts; I'm anything but beige.)

2. Keep the paragraphs short. Eliminate any unnecessary words. Readers read from top left to bottom right. (scanning)

3. Don't make the post too long. Readers are impatient. Get to the point. If it must be long, to get all the information in, at least break it up into sections or lists. And be sure to vary your sentence lengths just as you would do in stories. (See what I did there?)

4. Be human in your posts, not clinical. Let your personality shine through. It doesn't have to be filled with a myriad of superfluous verbiage … oops, did I just do that? Just be yourself.

5. Edit, edit, edit. Read your post, line for line, looking for typos. Nothing turns a visitor away from a blog (especially one aimed at "teaching" something) faster than a page full of grammatical errors.

6. Use at least three high-quality images in each post, as well as one for the "featured image." Make sure the featured image resonates with your post theme because it's the one people will see on the home page usually.

7. Space between your paragraphs. Don't allow the text to run together. And make sure your paragraphs keep the same theme. Start a new paragraph when you start a new supporting topic.

8. End your post with a call to action—a thought-provoking question, a compelling statement, or a link where they can learn more about that topic, or you in general.

9. Respond to your commenters, even if they are rude. Thank them for stopping by to share their thoughts, and address their comments in a professional manner. Don't engage in childish bickering; take the high road.

10. Most importantly, stay aware that not everyone who visits your site will agree with your posts. When you put your words out there for the world to judge, you must be willing to take the good and bad feedback. Remember that it's not personal, and people are much braver when they can hide behind a keyboard. Just be professional, state the facts (or your opinion if that's the type of blog you run), and set an example of how a professional blogger should behave.

Don't gauge your success in how many comments you receive on your posts, by the way. Many of my readers email me personally or respond on social media to let me know how much they enjoy my posts, but they don't comment on my blog. I don't care how I reach my readers, as long as the information I offer, helps them. That's my ultimate goal in blogging.

I wish you all much blogging success, many pleasant comments, and an abundance of followers.

A company contacted me recently about blogging services, and I found it quite interesting. These people train you on how to set up a website or blog, operate it, and grow your fan base.

Check out their site here: https://firstsiteguide.com/

TIP 298: 9 ways to trim blog-post creation time

Blogging takes up a great deal of time, from deciding what to blog about, to writing the content, to choosing the right images for each post.

Every blogger has his or her own unique routine and style of writing. Some are long-winded and provide extensive blog posts. Others like to get straight to the point. (That would be me.) But no matter what type of blogger you are, or what you blog about, the process can be quite time consuming.

Here are 9 ways to trim your time spent creating blog posts:

1. Always make sure to have at least three days' worth of blog posts scheduled. Emergencies and technology glitches happen. You don't want to risk being stuck in the middle of nowhere with no signal to be able to push your blog post through on time. Once you set a precedent with your readers/fans, you must do everything in your power to release your content on time as promised. Having several blog posts scheduled at one time can provide a huge relief in moments like these. A week's worth is even better.

2. Write all your content out first. Then go back and add font changes, edits, and images. Do not edit as you go.

3. Copy and paste your content to a Word document as a backup, just in case your computer shuts down or you lose Internet connection in the middle of a post. It's also a good idea to hit "save draft" or "update" as you go along, depending on if you've scheduled it or not yet. By the way, it's a good idea to go ahead and title your post and then

schedule it so you won't accidentally hit "publish" by mistake when you are trying to click "update" or "save draft."

4. Choose three to four images that relate to your post topic, and have them ready to copy and paste into your doc. It's even better if you save them to a file on your computer and upload them to your blog-platform media files. Think of keywords that relate most to your blog topic when choosing images.

5. Repurpose blog content and images occasionally.

6. Open your site/post in a new window to be able to simply change it in the editing window and click "update" as you go.

7. When you schedule the post, go ahead and choose the category and parameters you need, so it will show up in the correct place on the blog when it goes live.

8. Add the images last and set your featured image as you schedule the post.

9. Focus on your blog post. Don't open other windows and check social media updates or anything like that. Jump in and get it done. Then you can slide over to Facebook and check your messages.

Side tip: Always edit your blog posts carefully. Other than an offensive political comment, nothing turns a reader away from a blog post faster than finding a ton of grammatical issues. You are supposed to be an authority on writing. Why would your readers take advice from you if your posts are riddled with misspellings and content errors?

TIP 299: Blogging about your books
(increase exposure and sales)

We all know it takes a variety of marketing strategies to be a successful author these days. However, one way that truly connects with readers is blogging about your books.

Some authors blog as an aside from writing books because they have so many ideas and words floating around in their heads, they simply must release them. Others blog for fun, or to hone their writing skills. Whatever your reason for blogging, don't forget to plug your books on occasion.

Once your readers begin connecting with your content, whatever the niche, they may also be interested in delving into your longer writing pieces: your books.

Here are fourteen ways to blog about your books to increase sales:

1. Offer character interviews.

2. Offer images of your "envisioned" town or setting for one of your books. Tell the history of this place and why you chose it for your story, even if it's made up, but especially if it's a real town. You never know if some of your readers have a connection to this place.

3. Offer deleted scenes from your book. Readers love these!

4. Offer excerpts.

5. Show off your writing chops by offering a poem or short story based on a scene from your book or one of its characters.

6. Offer character bios and tell why you chose them. It helps to provide pictures of what you envision them to look like.

7. Share a little bit about how your story came to be, to allow readers into your thought/writing process. Was the story based on any "characters" in your real life? Did any events from the story happen to you personally? What made you write this story?

8. Offer a special, never-before-released short story, or an excerpt from your current WIP, only to your blog followers. Every so often, at random, choose one of your loyal followers and gift them a copy of one of your books—as a thank you.

9. Offer a perma-free book.

10. Hold contests with giveaways on your blog.

11. Use polls to get feedback on your current WIP – character names, names of towns in the story, etc. Readers enjoy being part of the creative process.

12. Conduct a virtual book tour.

13. Make sure your books are "clickable" for quick, easy purchase. Hyperlink the covers and offer each book its own page, or at the very least, a "my books" page. Be sure to offer ALL your buy links. The more places your book is available, the more opportunity you create for sales. You never know what device or platform readers use.

14. Make sure to offer your social media contact links so readers can connect with you outside of your blog, and share your content.

I wouldn't suggest mentioning your own books more than a couple times per month. Push other authors first, offer helpful content for your readers, and push your own work last. Humility will get you far in publishing, and life in general.

TIP 300: What to blog about ... besides books

I've seen this post many times on Facebook: "I just published my first book and I'm thinking of starting a blog (OR, my publisher said I should start a blog) but what should I blog about, besides my books?"

Most authors struggle with this problem at some point in their careers. Granted, many were avid bloggers *before* they published their books, but some have no clue how to get started or what to write about, much less how to create a site or operate a blogging program.

I can only speak on operating Word Press, as that's the only program I'm familiar with. If you have specific questions about that, feel free to email me at tsanderspublishing@yahoo.com.

Here are a few topics authors can blog about—besides (*or at least not always about*) their books.

For fellow writers: (These posts will help you network with other authors and possibly become a go-to for interviews, blog tours, or writing tips.)

- writing tips

- editing tips

- formatting for Kindle or Createspace (paperback)

- recommended editors, book cover designers, book trailer artists, illustrators, etc.,

- recommended writing software and tools

- recommended tutorial websites

- steps in the publishing process

- how to create well-developed characters and their backstories

- how to write a compelling book blurb, synopsis, or hook

- tips on outlining

- tips on networking

- tips on using social media to network and market your books (Pinterest, Facebook, Twitter, etc.,)

- tips on having a successful book signing

- things you would have done differently in your writing/publishing career

And the list goes on and on. I covered these topics and more in this segment thus far.

For readers/potential fans: (These posts help you connect with your readers/potential readers to expose your work, but to also let them know you are a real person, aside from your writing.)

- character interviews

- offer deleted scenes

- offer samples of your writing

- offer coupons or signed copies of your books

- interview/recommend other authors via podcast or stationary posts

- list your top twenty (fifty) classic novels as recommendations

- video book reviews

- share pictures of your book signings or your writing space (desk)

- talk about television programs that are similar to your books

- talk about the setting (central city) your books are based on – share pics of what you imagine it looks like, or authentic ones if it's a legitimate city

- share a few details from your WIP – pics of what you imagine the characters look like, a temporary cover, etc., – get cover ideas from your fans

**These posts don't have to be all about your books. You can offer a segment on healthy foods or exercises, if that's what you have experience with, and you can gain new followers simply by having something in common with others who are on the same journey. Compelling writing doesn't have to be fiction. So, if you decided later to publish a book about a general topic, some might buy it, based on your writing skills they were exposed to in your blog posts. It's about your writing talent and your personality, not your books.

General audience: (Authors are typically multi-talented. Perhaps they can cook, decorate or renovate homes or furniture, teach yoga, etc., Readers don't only read to escape. They read to learn new things.)

- how-to posts

- lists – things to do/not do while …

- If you have a big project that you're working on or planning, let your viewers follow you on that journey via videos or posts.

- review products you've bought and tried – not books

- problem-solution posts

- daily inspirational posts – could be quotes or unique writing

- surveys and polls

- trivia or quizzes – thought-provoking posts

- funny jokes or satirical posts

If you are a true writer, once you've chosen a theme, the ideas should flow easily, at least in the beginning. And, as they say, "a book always begins with a single word." Therefore, you can take all the posts you submit for one theme and create a book with them. That could be a long-term goal for your short-term blogging endeavors.

TIP 301: Quality vs. quantity – don't short change your readers

I've frequently heard questions like: How long should my novel or blog post be? Is there a word limit I should adhere to?

There is no right or wrong answer here. The ultimate truth is, quality always trumps quantity. Regardless of how long or short your articles, books, and posts are, make sure every word counts and moves your story or topic forward.

It takes what it takes.

If a blog article is discussing "Seven Mistakes New Authors Make," all seven must be listed, or you are shortchanging your readers.

With books, you must categorize your book as a short read, novella, or novelette accordingly on buy sites. It doesn't bother me if an author refers to his or her "novelette" as a novel in social interactions, because I always check the page count on Amazon, as do many other readers, to see what they are getting into. But be sure to categorize it correctly in genre and description.

Here are a few tips to ensure you always produce quality material:

1. Offer something of value or at least something that hasn't been done to death.

2. Use bullets for listed items for neat presentation.

3. Avoid unnecessary repetition.

4. Include quality images that relate to your blog posts.

5. Be original in your ideas and writing.

6. Write as if you are writing to your one ultimate reader.

7. Avoid using big words when simpler ones will do.

Avid readers can spot contrived blog posts and novel plots a mile away. Make sure what you have to say doesn't get lost in a sea of mediocrity.

TIP 302: Book bloggers and authors (a match made in book heaven)

It's no secret that book bloggers have become huge supporters of authors they like. A great review from a well-known book blogger can catapult an author into success, concerning sales and rankings, quite rapidly. I've seen it happen to author friends of mine!

When you connect with a book blogger who likes your writing style, word about your books can spread like wildfire, and you can gain new loyal followers in the process. Readers buy books based on recommendations of friends whose opinions they respect. Fact.

Therefore, one way to get your name out there as an author is to connect with book bloggers. But you must take the time to prepare what you will say and how you will say it. Prominent book bloggers are inundated with requests for book reviews, so they are quite choosy about their next reads. They have to be.

Many times, book bloggers won't even entertain the thought of reviewing an Indie book; however, there are tons who only review Indie books and are huge supporters of the Indie industry.

No matter which book blogger you choose, there are a few things to keep in mind when contacting one: (In the interest of eliminating wordiness, I'm going to refer to the blogger as a "her.")

1. Read over her site. Find out who this blogger is (as much as possible – some are quite private). What is her family life like? What are her other hobbies? What genres does

she read? Most book bloggers have a life outside of reading books. Some are authors as well.

2. Read over the blogger's submission requirements carefully. Don't waste time (hers or yours) submitting to one who doesn't read Indie books (if you are an Indie author). Follow the instructions explicitly when contacting her. Some require you to fill out a form online with your book information. Others allow you to email them directly. Some don't allow attachments. Others do. Be sure to do your homework on this.

3. If possible, find out the book blogger's name so that when you go to make contact, you have an actual person to address rather than the dreaded "Dear reader" or "Dear Ma'am."

4. Be sure to mention something unique about this book blogger to let her know that you have taken the time to learn more about her. Mention a great review she did, or an article she wrote. What's really nice is when you mention a recent book she reviewed and how yours is similar. (Ex: I saw your five-star review for "book title" and thought you might enjoy my book "book title," which has similar elements, but a plot twist you won't see coming.)

5. Be sure to find out where the book blogger posts her reviews and what the policy is on bad reviews. Most of them will post to Amazon and Goodreads as well as their blogs, but some only post on the blogs. As well, most don't like to have "rules" to follow about reviewing and will state in the policy that you will receive an honest review no matter what. That's a chance that authors take when putting their work out there, good or bad.

I have had great luck in garnering reviews from several awesome book bloggers. In fact, I even received a couple of reviews from top Amazon reviewers. Though I don't recommend using form letters (basically templates) to contact these bloggers, I am offering a sample of what I sent to obtain reviews, just to give you a place to start. Remember to personalize it. You are selling YOU in this process, not a template.

Hello, Katie.

As a blogger/reviewer, it's not hard to imagine that you are bombarded daily by authors and companies wanting you to try out their products, so I won't waste your valuable time.

Unsevered is a contemporary romance novel with some paranormal elements about a young military couple, Harley and Jewel. Harley is called to active duty in the Middle East immediately after the couple returns from their honeymoon. Jewel is unable to cope and begins losing touch with reality, until Harley visits her from the beyond with a message. If you enjoyed the movie, *GHOST*, you'll love *Unsevered*.

My ultimate goal in writing is to tell a good story and evoke emotions from my readers. Judging by the consensus of reviewers' sentiments thus far, this book accomplishes that goal, maintaining a 4.8 out of 5 stars ranking.

If you happen to find yourself in the mood for an emotional, compelling love story, I'd be honored for you to add *Unsevered* to your reading list.

Here is the pertinent information to help you locate my book with ease:

Title: *Unsevered*
Author: Traci Sanders

Length: 136 pages
Genre: Romance/Magical Realism
ASIN: B014FWLMQ4
Publication date: August 31, 2015

Below is a link where you can read an excerpt of *Unsevered* if you wish.

Unsevered teaser

If you would like a review copy, I would be happy to send one.

Thank you so much for your time and consideration of my work. Please feel free to respond with any questions you may have.

http://awordwithtraci.com/teaser-for-unsevered/

Best regards,
Traci Sanders

I wish you all the best of luck, new blogger friendships, and many future sales!

TIP 303: 3 types of virtual blog tours

There are a few different ways an author can contribute to a virtual blog tour. (Some also call it a virtual book tour.) No matter which type an author chooses to promote his or her book, the one thing they all have in common is: the success of the tour is dependent upon both the author and host working together.

Basically, there are three main types of virtual tours. The one you choose depends on what you are most comfortable with and how much you are able to commit to.

Option One: (an author hosts a tour on his/her blog – great for networking and drawing traffic to the blog)

In this case, the author hosting the tour invites other authors and readers to his/her own blog each day during a certain time frame – usually a month or a week – to introduce them to fellow authors.

More traffic for the blog will result if the guest author also promotes the tour. This is like a one-stop shopping experience for readers looking for a new book as well. It's easy for visitors because everything is conducted in one central location.

If you are not comfortable with blogging or networking, you would not want to choose option one, especially if you don't have a week or a month to dedicate to the tour to support the featured authors and visitors.

For this type of tour to be successful, you must have the following in place:

- A blog/site where you intend to hold the tour.

- A group of authors who you wish to feature – each author will need to submit material for his/her day including book cover images, author bio, book blurb and/or excerpt, buy links, contact links, and an author image.

- A set time frame in which you intend to hold the tour. Most authors do a week-long tour, but some do month-long spans.

- Each author participating needs to be (somewhat) present during his/her day to interact with the visitors – much like a regular party, but online, so the author can show up sporadically.

Option two: (the author sets up his/her own multi-blog tour – great way to develop new blogger relationships for fan-base expansion and future promotion)

Otherwise known as the blog-hopping tour, this would be the most outreaching one because you (as the featured author) would be connecting with a multitude of different bloggers, who in turn expose you to their readers. This option is quite time consuming and requires great detail to organization because you (as the featured author) would be responsible for keeping up with which blogs you are appearing on during certain days, as well as having to create various blog-post material for each one, since you will be directing your followers to each site. They will not be interested in reading the same book blurb or excerpt at each blog stop.

For this type of blog tour to be a success, you (the author) must have the following in place:

- A set time frame for the tour and a list of bloggers who are willing to host you for specific days. Again, most authors do a week-long tour, but some do month-long.

- Since your work will be featured on a different blog each time, you will need to have varied content ready to offer your readers (and potential new readers). You can offer character interviews, varied excerpts, or even samples of your other writing. But if you are trying to promote a certain book, you will want to stick with information about that book.

- You will need to do most of the promoting for the tour by letting your readers know what blogs you will be featured on, and on what days. You can ask the blogger hosts to help promote as well, but don't expect much unless you are good friends.

- You must be willing and able to visit each blog on the tour and interact with the visitors in some way. It's quite time consuming but great for networking.

Option Three: (an author is invited by a blogger to be featured along with a multitude of authors in a tour – usually only happens if the author is part of a like-minded group or has a relationship with a blogger who invites him or her.)

An author can participate in a pre-organized multi-blog tour. It's similar to option one, but in this case, the one who organized the tour does most of the back-end work and the featured author simply submits his/her blog post content and shows up for a specified day. This process draws more traffic to the host's site for each day a different guest author appears. The host will be promoting the entire tour, but the featured author will want to promote his/her special day as well.

For this tour to be successful, you will need to have a great content page – book cover, author bio and pic, book excerpt, maybe even a trailer if you have one, since you will be in a mix of other authors ... perhaps even some in your same genre. Therefore, you may want to consider offering something extra special – maybe a deleted scene or a character interview.

***Most featured authors offer some type of perk, such as a free copy of his/her book, or book swag, or a gift card of some sort.

Others may just set the price of their books at 99 cents for the duration of the tour.

I have personally participated in two types of blog tours. I've hosted a multi-author tour, and I've been featured in one. I've yet to set up my own tour on multiple blogs. It's a time-consuming task that requires a great deal of organization and commitment. I do have author friends who have been quite successful in this, however.

No matter which type you choose, virtual tours can be a lucrative endeavor if the author is willing to put in the time. New blogger relationships can be formed, book sales can be obtained, and new reader relationships can be developed—all good things for authors.

Happy touring!

TIP 304: No comment (blogging etiquette for readers)

Bloggers and readers have an unspoken dance, and it takes two for each dance (blog post). If one falls out of step, or doesn't reciprocate, the other feels all alone on the dance floor.

Bloggers post an article, then the readers like, share, or comment on that blog. That is the dance. Only, many times, bloggers feel as if they are grooving along solo and their partners never even showed up.

If you are a blog hopper and you enjoy reading various posts by your favorite bloggers, be sure to support his or her efforts by getting involved. We're all busy, this is true. However, if you take the time to read the post, remember to take the time to thank the blogger for the information.

Many times, great bloggers who offer informative and important posts stop blogging, or don't blog as often, because they don't receive any feedback. They feel as if they are talking to an empty room, as if what they are offering isn't needed as much as they'd thought.

Blog posts (good ones, anyway) take a great deal of time and sometimes money to produce. I spend between 30-45 minutes per blog post. Not only do I have to write the material, I also spend time searching for the perfect images to accompany my words. I research information to ensure accuracy of my content as well. It's a time-consuming endeavor, but one I enjoy. I receive personal messages via email and social media from my readers, so I know I'm not talking to an empty room. But I blog not just to offer information; I enjoy interacting with my readers.

If you want to keep your favorite bloggers writing, please support their efforts by doing one or all of these things:

1. Like the post.

2. Share the post on social media.

3. Comment on the post. Even a simple "thanks for the information" or "good tip" will suffice. Just as authors get paid in reviews and book sales; bloggers get paid in comments, shares, and likes.

4. Interact with the blogger – connect with him/her on social media.

5. Subscribe to the blogger's newsletter or blog.

6. If the blogger is an author, share his/her book links, or buy and review his/her books.

7. Enter the blogger's giveaways and share them on social media.

8. If the blogger has affiliate ads/links on the blog, shop through those links rather than direct shopping (for example, on Amazon).

9. Send a personal email to thank them for their time and efforts.

10. Offer blog topics. Professional bloggers don't really experience writers' block per se, but they do worry they are repeating information. Feel free to offer topics YOU'D like to see covered! Personally, I can write about almost anything, as long as I have a topic.

If you want to continue seeing posts by your favorite bloggers, send a little love their way. You don't have to agree with the blogger's post. You can share your thoughts without being rude. Constructive criticism helps bloggers grow and produce better content, just as with writing books.

After You Publish Part 4
All About Reviews

TIP 305: 7 reasons why friends/family don't review your books

Ah, the "elusive" friend/family book review. The funny thing about this concept is that you almost *expect* your "peeps" to be the first ones to not only run out (or go online) and buy your book, but review it right away—simply because of your relationship with them—and/or the fact that you have taken the time to check out (and spend money on) their Mary Kay, Avon, Amway, and other money-making endeavors, to help them out in the past. But in reality, it doesn't happen this way.

See, some of your "peeps" WILL buy your book and sing its praises to everyone they come in contact with.

Some will say they *love* it but never "get around" to posting a review for it.

Then, there are others who will never read it or review it, no matter how much they love YOU. I have come to accept that it's not a personal attack on me or my book.

Here are seven reasons why friends/family members choose not to read/review your books.

1. They are afraid they won't enjoy the book and do not want to have to deal with telling you so—and/or they don't want to lie in a review.

2. They enjoyed the book but they just aren't *writers*. They don't usually write reviews for anything—unless it earns them money or they are UNSATISFIED with a product ... that's when you'll really see their reviews online.

3. They are just "too busy" to take the time to get online, log-in to their account, find your book, and then post a review. *It is quite a process to go through*, and most people want everything to be done in one click—hence, why Amazon designed the "one-click" purchase option ... they don't give you time to change your mind or hesitate.

4. They aren't readers. Many people aren't. You will not find many books in their homes. Some people get headaches when they read. Others get sleepy. I know people who have said things like this. Some people can't even sit still long enough to read a book. Some just don't ... (gasp) ... enjoy reading!

5. They aren't interested in your book topic. Everyone has preferences and they are entitled to those. If you write children's books or non-fiction self-help books, some people may not be interested in what you have to say—or they may not *need* that information because that stage of their life is over.

6. They are not tech-savvy or computer literate. Some people still have no electronic devices in their homes—other than those that are necessary. It may sound unbelievable, but there are still millions of people who DON'T have smart phones, tablets, e-readers, laptops, etc. Often, these people, if they are readers, will ask for a paperback copy of your book. It's a good idea to keep paperbacks on hand.

7. They don't have an Amazon or Goodreads account and don't want to open one. This has been the case a few times for me. And don't bother trying to *explain* to them how to open one. People tend to resist things they aren't comfortable with, or have to take the time to learn about.

So, there you have it. Seven—legitimate or not (matter of opinion)—reasons why friends/family don't buy your books or review them.

I have learned to STOP asking. Once they know what you write and where and how to get it—IF they want it, they will go find it. Let it go for now.

It takes time for some people to come around. People are all about "social proof" these days. Once they see your ratings going up, your number of reviews increasing, and your sales totals growing, they MAY take a chance on you. Some will even, with false interest of course, ask you about your books *when they run in to you*. You will soon learn if these people are just asking to be nice and make conversation or if they really want to know. If they say things like, "Where can I buy it?" or "What is it about?" Chances are, they MAY want to know more. But if they simply ask, "How are your books going?" Just smile and politely say, "It's going great! I love being a writer," and leave it at that.

TIP 306: Resources to encourage more reviews for your books

One of the most frequent comments I hear from authors is, "I need more reviews." Authors know that although reviews don't necessarily *sell* books, they do encourage readers to learn more about a potential purchase. Reviews help readers *decide* whether or not to buy a book.

Having said that, reviews (real ones, anyway) are not easy to come by these days, due to the overflow of books available.

There are a few ways an author can go about getting reviews, other than begging friends and family for the umpteenth time.

One of the reasons many readers don't leave reviews is that they aren't quite sure about what to write. They are not writers, and some prefer to enjoy a good book in solitude and anonymity.

I recently created a couple of documents that have been well-received by my fellow authors, so I'm sharing them here. These were created for the readers who "just don't know what to write" in a review.

Fiction Book Review Cheat Sheet

Reviews are a crucial aspect of the writing process. Authors read them to learn what readers look for in a story so they can continue to write the stories readers will enjoy. We need your honest thoughts about our stories.

Authors realize that most people who review a book are not writers and may not know what to write, so we have come up with a way to simplify the review-writing process for you.

Feel free to use this cheat sheet provided. You can print it out or simply use it as a guide.
Fill out all or only a few select lines of text.
But PLEASE leave a review for the book you just read.

Reviews keep authors writing!

∞

The first thing that drew me in to this book was:

My favorite character was:
I liked this character because:

My least favorite character was:
I didn't like this character because:

My favorite part of the story was:

My least favorite part of the story was:

I would recommend this book to a friend   Yes   No

Why or why not? (if you would like to explain)

Nonfiction Book Review Cheat Sheet

Reviews are a crucial aspect of the writing process. Authors read them to learn what readers look for in a book so they can continue to write the books readers will enjoy. We need your honest thoughts about our books.

Authors realize that most people who review a book are not writers and may not know what to write, so we have come up with a way to simplify the review-writing process for you.

Feel free to use this cheat sheet provided. You can print it out or simply use it as a guide.
Fill out all or only a few select lines of text.
But PLEASE leave a review for the book you just read.

Reviews keep authors writing!

∞

The first thing that drew me in to this book was:

What I found most helpful about this book was:

What I found least helpful about this book was:

Nonfiction topics I wish there were more books about are:

The author of this book was knowledgeable about the topic.   Yes   No

I would recommend this book to a friend   Yes   No

Why or why not? (if you would like to explain)

You all are welcome to tweak these to your needs and upload them into the back section of your books to encourage reviews. If you're unable to retrieve them as pictures here, feel free to email me at tsanderspublishing@yahoo.com and I'm happy to send copies.

Another resource for authors in getting real reviews is a site I created, along with a great team of authors and readers. It's called Readers Review Room.

Here is how it works:

1. An author submits his/her buy links to our vetting team at readersreviewroom@gmail.com.

2. As a team, we vet the title for likability, flow, and grammatical and formatting issues. A title doesn't have to be perfect. It simply has to have a story that catches our attention, and have no glaring formatting or grammatical issues. But if the sample is loaded with head-hopping, tense changes, and grammatical issues, we decline it.

3. If a title is declined, we offer improvement suggestions and an invitation to resubmit once these changes have been made.

4. If a title is approved, we invite the author to list it with us to make it available for our reviewers to choose from. We list up to 3 titles for just $9.95/year or unlimited titles for just $14.95/year. (These prices are subject to change over time.)

5. Once listed, a title is available for any of our reviewers to pick up at their discretion. The reviewer notifies me of his/her choice and he/she has up to 30 days to submit a review for that title (or longer if needed). I announce the picked-up title on our FB and Twitter pages, and try to tag the author so he/she can keep up with the progress as well.

6. When one of our team members offer a review, he/she also offers a rating image that is unique to our site—a bookworm.
    We have 3 bookworm ratings: Gold (equivalent to 5 stars),

Blue (equivalent to 4 stars), and Green (equivalent to 3 stars).

Along with a worm rating, our reviewers offer honest, thoughtful reviews that allow a reader to really know what he/she is getting with that title—unbiased feedback that authors need.

7. We share all reviews on our social media pages.

8. In addition to posting reviews by the RRR team, we also now offer "other" reviews to be posted for titles. Authors are responsible for contacting individuals who have reviewed their books and having them submit their reviews to us at readersreviewroom@gmail.com. We will vet the review for authenticity and make sure the reviewer actually read the book. If it's legitimate, we will add it as an "other reviewer" review on the title's page.

At this moment, we have more than 230 titles from 100 different authors on the site, and we're always adding to our library. Come check them out at readersreviewroom.com.

**Note: Our reviewers are not influenced personally or professionally in their feedback and choose titles on their own accord. Please do not submit your title to us if you are not willing to receive honest feedback on it, whether from our vetting team or our reviewers.

I'm happy to answer any questions you all may have about the review cheat sheets or the Readers Review Room. These are just guidelines to get authors thinking outside the box when vying for reviews. Please come back and share your results, if you're able to see a difference after implementing any of these resources.

TIP 307: How to handle low-star reviews (and why 5-star reviews aren't always best)

Amazon has set authors up to believe that reviews are the be-all and end-all of success in the publishing industry, other than book sales. There have even been rumors circling the web that magical things are supposed to happen when a book attains fifty reviews. In my personal experience, this is simply not true. I've even confirmed this with other Indie authors who have hundreds of reviews for their books.

My findings: reviews don't increase book sales, and customers don't care as much about "verified reviews" as Amazon would like to convince us they do.

With that said, reviews are important for 4 *other* reasons:

1. They allow feedback for authors, letting them know what works and doesn't work for their target audience.

2. They allow readers a chance to thank or offer suggestions to an author.

3. They allow potential customers to make an informed decision about book purchases. (I personally would have never known what a verified purchase was if I'd not researched it when I first published. That factor never affected what books I bought as a reader.)

4. The more reviews a book has, good or bad, verified purchase or not, the more likely a reader will take a chance on it.

As we are all aware, Amazon has a star-based review system in place for books (and other products, but we will focus on books here). The ratings range from 1-star being the lowest and 5-stars being the highest. They don't offer a deeper explanation of the stars; it's simply set up like a school grading system.

Many times, authors will get upset or discouraged by a low-star rating, because we all want 5 stars, right? Well, from everything I've learned about the review system, we shouldn't be striving for all 5-star ratings. Of course, we don't want all 1-star ratings either. But contrary to what Amazon, or many industry professionals would try to have you believe, a 3-star rating is NOT that bad.

I've seen books receive 3-star ratings (or lower) for various reasons:

1. poor editing

2. lack of connection to the characters

3. lack of connection to the story line

4. the story wasn't in the reader's preferred genre (not his or her cup of tea)

5. offensive scenes or language

6. the book was too short

7. the book was too long

8. the story was too slow

9. the story was too fast

The list can go on and on because each reader offers a different perspective on the story. Many readers check out existing reviews for a book to compare their thoughts and feelings to others' sentiments. I personally have read books that I did not care for at all, and often could barely finish. But when I checked out the other reviews for those books, they were all four and five stars. It baffled me.

So, what is an author to do if he/she receives a low-star rating?

NOTHING!

It's more about what you SHOULD NOT do.

1. Do not write the reviewer to ask for an explanation. You may be further offended by the answer, or the reviewer may block you or take to social media to label you as a stalker or complainer.

2. Do not comment on the review, other than to say, "Thank you for taking the time to share your thoughts on my book." Even then, only do this if you know the reviewer well enough to know he/she doesn't mind it. Some reviewers like to remain anonymous.

3. Do not take to social media and badmouth the reviewer. You never know who he/she is friends with.

4. Do not contact Amazon or the review site to complain about the reviewer. It will get you nowhere.

5. Do not stop writing because of an unfavorable review.

What you CAN do:

1. If you receive several similar reviews for your books, you may need to take another look at them. Have a professional editor work on them if the reviews mentioned typos. You may have missed a few things the first time.

2. Without mentioning the name of the reviewer, vent or talk to a fellow author who has been in your position,

preferably one who is more experienced than you and is not a negative person.

3. Make a goal to produce a better book next time. Learn the craft and ensure each subsequent book is better than the last.

4. Take a writing or editing course to hone your craft.

5. Read lots of books in your genre and compare them to yours to see if you can strengthen your own writing.

6. Exercise to get some stress out – kickboxing, aerobics, running, etc.

7. Punch a pillow. Scream. Squeeze a stress ball.

8. Write a nasty comment or response to the reviewer in Word. Then delete it!

Reviews are the best way for authors to gauge their writing skills, **but a less-than-stellar review does not mean you're a terrible writer,** as I mentioned above. If I see a book that has all 5-star reviews, it makes me suspicious. As well, if I see one that has all low-star reviews, I will probably not take the time to dig further. A good mix of various star ratings is the best way to gauge authenticity of the book's quality. I always pick one or two low ratings and one or two high ratings to read to help me decide whether or not I will purchase a book.

And even as an author, my goal is not to get all 5-star ratings; I simply want honest feedback from my readers. I want to know how my words made them feel. That's my ultimate payoff.

Here is a thought on this topic, by Stephen Geez:

I think several points are important to keep in mind. If you're looking at your reviews on Amazon, that location is a small subset of your readers, people who not only visit Amazon, but who have an account there. Some kinds of books are way more likely to garner any kind of reviews than others, mainly because some audience demographics are way more likely to post than others. I believe a book targeting YA or young mainstreamers will generate substantially more "postings" than a book targeting middle-agers. (I know older voracious readers who don't even have email accounts, let alone a track record of posting anything anywhere; and I know people who purchase from Amazon but don't see it as anything but a retailer, not a place for interaction.) Readers of literary works almost never post reviews while readers of pop genres such as thrillers and romance do. (A deeply detailed literary tale built on metaphor seems to call for a college-level lit paper to comment with equal depth and understanding, an intimidating proposition; while "I figured out the bad guy right away" or "I really hated her boyfriend but the guy at the hot-dog stand was way cool" is very easy to post by people who don't feel any more than that is expected of them.) Point is, your book, your genre, your readers–maybe they don't even visit Amazon, or don't post reviews, or don't post well-considered critiques as opposed to "I give this two stars because the woman it's about is such a bee-yotch." Some authors solicit readers to post reviews, while others consider that *déclassé*. I have letters from people who used the publisher address on the copyright page to send thoughtful, heartfelt sentiments about what a book of mine meant to them. Each of those will always mean more to me than a one-liner responding to Amazon's relentless "Rate your purchase" emails.

So, keep reviews in perspective. Don't be discouraged by a decided lack of them. Don't be inflated by a pile of short-and-shallows. Don't let Amazon make you forget your audience might well prefer to get its books through other outlets.

And consider this: how many potential buyers consider even the average-star rating, how many look at reviews, and how many of that subset read more than, say, five? What are 350 reviews worth? It looks like at least 350 people read the book, but most people understand it doesn't even mean that.

While writing this I've been emailed three times by Amazon pestering me to "review" books I recently bought but aren't even close to reading yet. I'd rather be so moved by a book that I seek out a way to say what I thought, not be hounded into it.

Remember that, too.

TIP 308: How to write solid Amazon reviews

Authors are typically more concerned with how to *obtain* great reviews on Amazon than how to write them. However, most writers are readers before they become published authors, and many continue to be avid readers long after. Therefore, it makes sense that these same authors will leave reviews for the books they read.

One perk to being a consistent reviewer on Amazon is, the more reviews one submits, the higher one's Amazon reviewer ranking is. Why is this important?

The answer is simple. The closer to the top 10,000 of Amazon's reviewer list a person gets, the higher the chances are of companies and other authors contacting that person to review their products/books.

And …

It eventually comes full circle. The more reviews you submit as a top Amazon reviewer, more people start taking notice of your books and view you as an established author. Also, Amazon puts a great deal of stock into your reviews, and there is less chance of any of them being removed.

That being said, this post is for authors and readers … basically anyone who doesn't want his/her reviews to be removed from Amazon for breaking the "personal relationship" rule.

Here are ten things to remember when submitting a review:

1. If you purchased the book from Amazon, the chances of your review being deleted are not as high. (Be aware, it can

still be removed. I've had two removed because of the "personal relationship" rule.)

2. A few years ago, if you were gifted a book, you would state that in the review that you received the book in exchange for your honest thoughts. Now, this is a no-no! It's best to not even mention how or why you attained the book. Also, don't say something like, "My cousin is the author of this book and I couldn't wait to read it." Family members and close friends are not allowed to review our books.

3. In your review, try to avoid the typical "red flags" that Amazon looks for:
I couldn't put this book down.
It was so great.
I met this author in a book club.
This author is so sweet; I'm so proud of her. (Don't reveal anything that could hint you know the author personally.)

4. Try to mention one or two specific lines that you enjoyed from the book to prove that you actually read it. The best way to do this is to use the "highlight" or "note-taking" feature on your Kindle to bookmark certain lines you liked. Then you can go through them later and choose the best one.

5. Read the other reviews for the book to make sure you are not repeating the same statements.

6. Choose a catchy, unique title for your review—one that stands out from the others.

7. Write more than just three or four lines. Amazon wants to know that you read this book and you are qualified to give an honest opinion on it.

8. Don't give every book you read five stars; Amazon and other potential readers will think you aren't an honest reviewer.

9. DO NOT put a link to your own book, or any other author's book in your review. That's an automatic deletion most of the time.

10. Don't retell the author's story or offer spoilers. Authors don't appreciate it; nor do readers.

Reviews take time, and are the bread and butter for authors, especially Indie authors. The last thing a reader or author wants is for a review to be deleted for "not seeming legitimate."

Follow these guidelines to keep your reviews safe from elimination.

TIP 309: Reviews aren't just for books

By now, I'm sure you now realize how important reviews are for authors. Reviews give us feedback on our writing and keep us motivated to write more. However, reviews are just as important to other types of artists and businesses.

I rarely buy anything, especially online, without checking the ratings and reviews for it. The same is true when traveling out of town and checking out hotels, restaurants, etc.

Reviews provide inside information on people, products, and businesses, and can save us a great deal of time and money.

Did you buy a new charger for your Samsung laptop recently? Were you satisfied with its performance? Why not share your experience with that product to help someone else out?

Here are just a few types of entities one can review:

1. online stores

2. restaurants

3. retail shops

4. download sites – software, music, etc.

5. services sites – Fiverr, editing and proofreading services, book-cover designers, etc.

6. airlines

7. hotels

8. auto-rental services

9. cab services

10. salons

11. bridal shops

12. bakeries

13. utility services

14. vehicle-repair shops

The list goes on and on.

As you may already know, most customers check the bad reviews before the good ones. They want to know what's "wrong" with a product, service, or business first and foremost because, let's face it, no one wants to waste time or money. It's no fun to plan an exciting night out to dinner with your loved one, only to receive poor service and terrible food. It can ruin the entire night.

Another benefit to submitting reviews for things other than books (on Amazon, anyway) is that you will be recognized as a "genuine reviewer" and Amazon will not delete or bar your reviews.

Most authors use a variety of services in their writing/publishing process, and many of them are based online. So why not help a fellow author (or shopper) out by sharing your experience in a review? Surely, you'd want the same done for you.

After You Publish Part 5
Genre-Specific Marketing

TIP 310: (For romance authors)
13 tips on writing love scenes

**Warning: This tip is intended for a mature (18+) audience. It is not for the faint of heart or virginal ears that are easily offended either. (smile)

Okay, guys. Being that I'm a romance author and avid romance reader, I'm going to share some tips on how to write a tasteful-yet-engaging love scene.

Achieving this is not as easy as one might think, and many authors do romance novels a great disservice by not taking the time to learn how to craft a classy love scene. This does not pertain as much to erotica, as we all know exactly what to expect in those books.

In fact, I will go ahead and define what I consider to be the difference between romance and erotica, as there are many preconceived notions about both.

Romance: has more story than sex and follows a main story theme

Erotica: has more sex than story but still has a main story theme (though it's not quite as clearly defined). I call it "book porn" but that doesn't make it true pornography, which has almost no story and definitely not much emotion.

Both genres have their places in the literary world. In fact, I commend authors who are bold and brave enough to venture into that arena. Many erotica stories are considered smut (or trash)—depending on the reader. However, my thought on this is: sex is a natural part of life. To coin a phrase from a popular movie from the 90s (I won't say which one), "We all do it; it's just that no one talks about it."

Well, erotica authors, and some romance writers, are brave enough to *talk* about what some others aren't.

Then, of course, there is the third category: hard-core porn, which belongs mostly in certain magazines and on websites that are adult rated, not so much in books. But, that's just my opinion.

Moving on …

Here are some tips for writing a sexy love scene:

1. Before you write the scene, envision what the characters look like—their hair and eye colors, what they are wearing, etc.

2. Keep in mind the characters' personalities. Is she submissive? Is he domineering? Does she have body-image issues? Things of that nature. If she's ashamed of her body, chances are, she would not react well to having sex in the middle of an open field in broad daylight without some interesting comments (dialogue) going on.

3. Make sure the dialogue and prior events create a nice flow into the sexual moment. It's best when it happens naturally rather than the two just ripping one another's clothes off. There may be laughing, small injuries from bumping into things, or fumbling with clothing.

4. Envision the setting. Are they outside, in their bedroom, in a car, on the beach? Make sure to set the mood with the setting. Is the moon out? Is it first thing in the morning?

5. Keep in mind that you don't have to tell every little move a character makes. You don't have to say *she stood and then walked over to him*, unless it's absolutely necessary, or *he unbuttoned his pants and then unzipped them*. Duh! The main thing a reader looks for in a romance novel is the escapism, not a play by play of the same things she does at least once a week with her spouse. (Two times a week?

Three?) Anyway, you get the picture. Oh, and you don't have to mention the whole condom application thing or especially the disposal of said condom.

6. Avoid using adjectives and adverbs that paint unpleasant pictures in readers' minds. Examples would be: moist, squirt, swollen, puffy, squishy, etc.

7. Avoid using anatomically correct terms to describe genitalia such as: vagina, scrotum, testicles, penis, labia, ejaculate, masturbate, semen, … you get the point.

8. Use as many senses as possible – touch, taste, sight, hearing, and scent – to bring readers into the moment with the characters.

9. Use vivid body language – not just walked, stood, sat, scooted, jumped, etc. Use words like slid, danced, trailed, fumbled, ripped, lingered, scratched, dug, pressed, cried, moaned, gasped, inhaled deep, etc.

10. Add sexy props to the scene – food, lingerie, pillows, blindfolds, bathtub/shower, wall, etc. Don't make everything about the bed.

11. Make sure the sex scene shows an emotional connection of some sort between the characters. Or, at the very least, make sure it moves the story forward somehow and has a purpose. In fact, every scene in a story should have a purpose.

12. Tease your readers instead of spelling everything out. Allow their imaginations to fill in the gaps.

13. Don't overdo the frequency of sex scenes. In other words, don't offer a sex scene for each time the characters are alone together. It's not believable and can often seem repetitive to the readers. As well, it's not easy to write

several different sex scenes for the same characters and make each one unique.

Most importantly, keep your audience/genre in mind. Don't fill your story with multiple, gritty sex scenes and try to pass it off as romance. You may find a plethora of angry romance readers on your hands if so. Erotica has more "fudging" room so to speak when it comes to sex scenes, because its readers expect the dirty, gritty, sexy verbiage and graphic imagery.

Read your lines to yourself aloud. If you're too embarrassed to say it, chances are, you shouldn't be writing it.

TIP 311: Just what is considered clean fiction?

The terms "clean reads" and "clean fiction" have become more prevalent in the publishing industry in the past few years. Neither is a recognized, traditional genre, but more of a trendy one that has developed over time from the readers and authors of these particular books.

While I'm not here to preach to anyone or choose a side in this discussion, as I enjoy both genres, it's important to note there is a difference between clean fiction and Christian fiction.

Here are the characteristics of clean fiction:

- little to no swearing

- the characters have fairly high morals and values

- little to no violence

- discreet sexual content, mostly referenced rather than spelled out

- the primary purpose is to entertain the reader or help the reader escape, but it's not to persuade or inform readers about Christianity or religion of any type

Here are the characteristics of Christian fiction:

- no violence or swearing, or it's possibly downplayed and not very descriptive/graphic

- the main purpose is to offer spiritual-based content or scripture, or possibly even persuade readers through such content

- stories are written from a Christian world view

- often, a character, or many characters travel a path to spiritual revelation, maturation, or healing

Many Christian readers are often disappointed when they pick up a book categorized as Christian fiction, only to find mild swearing, suggestive-but-not-graphic sexual content, and possibly morally-challenged characters doing things they would consider "worldly" or sinful. The Christian genre has become a hot spot for many aspiring clean-fiction writers, whose books are incorrectly categorized in this way.

In summation, whether you are a reader or a writer of clean fiction, be aware that you must tread carefully with your audience and make it known that your books are not considered Christian fiction. Many times, even Amazon will incorrectly categorize a book; therefore, it's up to the author to clarify any possible misunderstandings with readers.

State in the description if your book contains any sexual content, violence, swearing, or other non-Christian-like elements, and this will ensure you don't encounter disgruntled readers who were "offended" by your story's content not aligning with their beliefs and values.

Here are a couple comments from two of my blog followers, offering varying views on this topic:

A few of my novels have been "clean," though I have never—and never will—write anything that advocates any religious beliefs. The difference for me is intended audience. I can make what I hope are profound plunges into the depths of humanity without dwelling in areas that make some audiences uncomfortable, and for those readers when I do touch on "unclean," I make sure it's in a limited and usually light-hearted way.

Dance of the Lights has, according to my fan mail, made many readers cry as they are drawn into some of the painful experiences of grief, but the only time it crosses into sexuality is a brief scene where two very old and injury-limited characters fool around maritally with only their fun banter as the focus, not the who-did-what-to-whom.

Quite the opposite, *What Sara Saw* is vivid in its harsh treatment of two children, in the nervous fantasies of two college-age innocents, and in the steps toward overcoming teenage trauma to learn new ways of understanding and pursuing intimacy. Still, how people think and feel and act is the focus in lieu of overly graphic descriptions. The blurb for *Sara* warns readers "Staggering revelations entangle them with issues of mortality and faith, sexuality and family violence, obligation and responsibility, deception and truth. Only by looking closely at the dark and profane will they have any chance of coming together to create a legacy more beautiful than either ever imagined." A description like this both warns those who might be too uncomfortable and attracts those who eschew "sanitized" fiction in favor of gritty tales that look unflinchingly at who we are.

In short, "clean" is not easily defined, so it's our job to write for the expectations of our intended audience, then to promote the work in ways that help people understand what to expect. I think about this a lot when I work on a project, so I'm glad to see it addressed here, as I can tell some writers are very careless about this. Thanks, Traci.
Stephen Geez

I'd also like to thank you for bringing up this subject, Traci.

I had an encounter in our group forum with an author who posted her book. When I took the post down and explained to her that one scene (in particular) was outside the rules of posting in our group, which are not strictly for Christian writing, but for clean (and I do mean absolutely clean, no foul language or explicit sexual descriptions) fiction.

Unfortunately, I had agreed to be a Beta reader for this author before I fully understood how she wrote. She got very angry with me, saying that Christians need to stop being "protected." She felt that young people need to know what happens in the "real world," and that I was being unfair. She wanted her children to read this.

The scene which made me take down the post for her book was one where child abuse was being explained without any doubt to what was happening. When I told her that my decision stood, she quit the forum, saying that I was "narrow-minded." Her writing, in my opinion, didn't fit into "clean fiction," although I know that there are others who also label their like-writing such.

Regarding, "Christian fiction," that is how I would label my writing, aside from the Christian/Romance/Suspense genre. I do have some violence written into the stories, but it's never perpetrated by the Christian character (although I know there have been acts of violence committed by Christians in real life). The Christian character may be drawn into the violence, or have to use force against it, but that's where I draw the line.

The most important thing I see in determining whether your story is Christian fiction or simply clean fiction is whether it has a spiritual message for the reader or not.
Sharon K. Connell

TIP 312: All about the kids

This tip is geared specifically for children's book writers. In addition to romance and parenting titles, I write children's books.

One of the biggest misconceptions about children's books is that they are easy to write. "You just throw a few cute words on the pages and some great illustrations, and voila!"

Not even close.

In my opinion, writing children's books is even more challenging than adult books for a few reasons:

1. Kids can be picky, and their parents even pickier.

2. It takes a great deal of time and money to produce a children's book—much more than most novels, because of the illustrations and formatting, and especially if you plan to publish in paperback.

3. Every word counts in a children's book because a line can be too cumbersome to read if it has too many big words, but a child can lose interest if the words aren't interesting enough.

4. Children's books are hard to sell to make your money back—even if they are traditionally published—because of the printing and packaging costs, and the market being flooded with them.

So, for those who have considered writing a children's book, be aware that there is not much money to be made unless you are a marketing genius, or you publish traditionally. I have self-published two children's books so far, but have six more that haven't gone to illustration yet simply because of what I went through financially and time-wise for my first two. I am considering getting my next ones traditionally published.

Also, not everyone can write quality children's books. With nearly twenty years of combined experience teaching toddlers and preschoolers, along with being a mom of three, I know what type of books, characters, and illustrations children enjoy. I also know how long they will typically sit for a book. I'm aware of how parents feel when reading certain books to their children, and some parents will refuse to buy certain books simply because "they" don't enjoy reading them.

With that said, here are a few tips for writing children's fiction:

1. Read. Read. Read. Just as with writing novels, reading books in your writing genre is crucial to understanding the word patterns and flow. Consider them study guides.

2. Remember what it was like to be a child. Get down on a child's level (mentally) and think about what type of books you enjoyed.

3. Write a unique character. Bears, rabbits and turtles have been done to death, in my opinion. My daycare children enjoy reading stories about unique animals such as raccoons, elephants, tigers, or even unicorns.

4. Read to your children, if you have little ones. Picture books are geared toward three to eight or ten years of age. Visit a local library or preschool and read to them. Learn how it takes inflection in your voice and pacing within the lines and pages. Children often ask a lot of questions during the reading. Learn how to write engaging, thought-provoking lines to encourage this.

5. If you plan to self-publish, you must find a good illustrator—one who will work within your timeline and budget. Expect it to take at least six months to have one book ready to purchase. Illustrations take time. If you plan to query agents, and you are an author/illustrator, you can work up a dummy book for them. But typically, they will use their own illustrators.

6. Join a children's critique group or submit your drafts to online mommy groups for approval or suggestions. Remember, children's books involve parents too. They are the ones purchasing (and typically reading) these books.

7. If you plan to submit to agents or publishers, be ready for rejections and revisions. Even if they accept your manuscript, chances are, they will use their own editors and illustrators. And many times, much of your work will be cut to fit industry standards.

8. Above all, remember why you are writing children's books. If you are a true children's author, you are not doing it for the money; you are writing to entertain children and encourage a love of the written word at an early age.

Be patient with your children's books. One title can take a year or more to be released. And even authors who secure agents or publishers for one of their books aren't guaranteed the same amount of representation for all their titles. It's not uncommon for publishers to reject other books by that same author. Publishers choose what they know they can sell. And even then, it sometimes falls flat.

Keep reading, writing, and making children smile with your words, and you will succeed!

Here are a few adorable children's titles by a very talented author and friend, Anita Kovacevic.

Here are the buy links:

Winky's Colours – available in paperback and Kindle

Mimi Finds Her Magic – Kindle

The Good Pirate – Kindle

Anita was spotlighted on Lulu! Learn more about her here: http://www.lulu.com/spotlight/Anita_K

If you'd like to check out my latest children's picture book *The Chocolate Monsters*, it's available for just 99 cents on Kindle! It's a rhyming story.

The Chocolate Monsters

TIP 313: 7 tips for children's books that rhyme

I've been advised by many professionals in the traditional publishing realm to avoid rhyming books at all costs. Years ago, I even queried an agent who wouldn't even look at my manuscript because she responded right away, politely stating that *the industry* doesn't look favorably upon rhyming books anymore, unless the book is written by Dr. Seuss.

I strongly disagree with that for a few reasons.

1. As an early educator for nearly twenty years, I can wholeheartedly state that most young children (who these books are written for) adore rhymes. They learn the words quickly and retain the information longer. I mean, even the ABC song is a rhyme, and that's one of the first songs a child learns.

2. Rhymes teach little ones about word play. If young children are exposed to rhyming books consistently, they learn how to assimilate the same ending sounds in both words. An epiphany moment occurs as a child might say, "Hey! *Cat* and *bat* sounds the same." Even if they don't realize what rhymes are, they learn the basic foundation of rhyming.

3. Rhymes make reading fun for kids. Many kids who grow up reading rhyming books become songwriters and poets in later years. I can personally attest to that.

But with that said, I will agree that rhyming is an art form and it must be done carefully, especially in books.

Many authors assume that just because they can write a great novel, or can write well period, that they can write a children's book. This is not true in all cases.

Rhyming is not easy!

Here are 7 things to keep in mind if you choose to write a rhyming book:

1. The rhymes must make sense with the story. In other words, don't throw the words *carousel* and *caramel* together … unless you have a unique story to tell. (See, I can't stop myself!) Seriously, choose a better word if possible. Also, keep in mind that people pronounce certain words differently, such as pecan and caramel. I'm sure you've heard it pronounced various ways.

2. Rhythm is just as important as the ending sounds. The best way to keep a rhythm is to tap it out or clap it out with your hands to make sure the text flows.

3. Every children's book doesn't have to rhyme. And every poem doesn't have to rhyme, as long as the story flows. You can rhyme just a few lines here and there. Kids enjoy that as well.

4. Don't use large words just because they rhyme with other words. Keep the rhymes simple. (*Aardvark* and *dark* may not be the best choices for a children's book.)

5. Some people mistake words that are spelled the same, as rhyming words. (Example: *toad* and *broad*) These are not rhyming words.

6. Read a lot of rhyming books before writing one. Practice a few lines and read them aloud to yourself or someone else, preferably a child.

7. Just because a line is approximately the same length, doesn't mean it will flow well. Reading it aloud is the only way to determine flow.

These are a few tips to get you started in writing rhyming books. Most of all, have fun with the words, and that will ensure the kids will have fun reading it.

Here is a comment on this topic, shared by Stephen Geez:

I know another: Fresh Ink Group. I'm proud to announce we published *The ABC's of Cancer for Kids* … featuring Cornelius the Cancer Fighting Crocodile. It's a rhymer getting rave reception from beta kids and sponsors who are writing checks to help the author sponsor it.

I really like *The Chocolate Monsters*, too. Of course, I'm only eight (um, and a half century).

Rhyming kid books is like rap music, in that it can be done to the level of art and it can be total dreck.

Thanks, Traci.
Stephen Geez

TIP 314: Marketing to young children and teens

This tip is about a topic I'm passionate about as a mom, and as an author. With so many movies, videos, and games at their fingertips, it's becoming increasingly difficult to encourage kids to read.

But that is why it's more important than ever to ensure that kids DO keep reading. They are our future reviewers, authors, editors, and publishers!

With schools getting rid of cursive writing, and "not counting off" for grammar or spelling issues in the younger grades, many kids are becoming lazy with their writing and grammar skills. Even worse, they are writing like they text. A majority of high school graduates are not even able to write a professional email.

Reading begins in the home. Parents should read to their young children to encourage a love of language. School-age kids should read for leisure, not just for assignments.

How do authors of children's books, middle-grade fiction, and YA fiction reach their audience?

Here are a few ways:

1. Visit local libraries and offer live readings. Perhaps you can work with the library manager to offer a "teen night" or something. Some teens do visit the library, and just don't let their friends know about it.

2. Visit local elementary, middle, and high schools to network with the teachers and see if they will allow you to offer copies of your books to the students who are interested in them. Ask those students to write reviews

you can share on your website (if age appropriate, of course).

3. Visit local colleges and see if they will allow you to leave copies of your books in their lounge or cafeteria. Or perhaps the English teachers will let their students know about your books.

4. Visit a local preschool or elementary class to see if the teacher will allow you to do a reading during show-and-tell or circle time. Teachers love classroom helpers.

5. Get a booth in school fundraiser functions, such as fall festivals. Many times, these events allow outsiders to rent a booth for their crafts or products.

6. If you have nieces, nephews, children, or grandchildren who would read for this age group, ask them to write a review you can share on your site. Also, ask their friends to check out your books and offer their thoughts.

7. One thing you can offer that might appeal to older kids is allowing them to review your book via a YouTube video. Kids these days are all about making videos of themselves. Get permission from their parents to post the video review on your site.

These are just a few ways authors of this genre can reach their target audience. You must think out of the norm to gain the attention of kids these days. You have to find where they are and go to them. Your book covers and themes must be intriguing because kids in this generation have short attention spans. Your characters must be relatable and engaging. If you think adult reviewers are harsh, try having a thirteen-year-old offer feedback on your book. Teens have no qualms in conveying their honest thoughts.

To begin this revolution of encouraging more young people to read, I've added two sections to the Readers Review Room site. (www.readersreviewroom.com)

One is called Rising Readers, where kids ages 8-12 can read age-appropriate books listed on our site and offer their honest thoughts in the form of reviews. I even coach them on how to set up their reviews and check their grammar, but I don't coach them on what to say.

The other section is called Teen Turf, where young people ages 13-19 can read age-appropriate books on our site and offer reviews as well. I even mark which books are for older teens by labeling them 16+, and no book is able to be checked out of the site without a parent's approval. We have a few teens on our team so far, but we're recruiting more.

So far, the initial appeal for these kids has been having their own review pages, but they are also enjoying our books. And the parents are excited about their kids reading!

If you are an author of these genres, and you are struggling to find your readers, feel free to send your buy links to readersreviewroom@gmail.com for vetting. If we list your titles, they will be available for any of our reviewers (including adults) to pick up at their own discretion.

TIP 315: How short should short fiction be?

More and more, short fiction is taking over the scene, (no pun intended), because readers always want great stories but don't always have the time to sit for an entire novel.

Short fiction can be classified in many different ways: (broken down into simple terms)

Vignette – a brief, evocative description, account, or episode (some vignettes are poems)
It can be a stand-alone piece or part of a larger work.

Example: *The House on Mango Street* by Sandra Cisneros

Vignette is a French word that means "little vine." During the nineteenth century, printers would decorate title pages with drawings of looping vines.

Literary sketch – basically a character sketch – has little or no plot, and can be accompanied by a drawing, but not necessarily
Example:
Accomplished news reporter Amber Woods is an auburn-haired beauty of medium build with emerald eyes. Her fiery temper is outmatched only by her big heart. She loves her family more than life itself, but also wants to be a role model for her children. Balancing her strong desire for personal and professional excellence with her domestic duties is her biggest struggle.

This concept was introduced after the sixteenth century in response to growing middle-class interest in social realism and foreign lands.

Story sequence – a group of short stories that collaborate to form a longer piece

Example: *Go Down, Moses* by William Faulkner

Mini saga – a story told in exactly fifty words

This type of writing tests a writer's skills in brevity with compelling details to convey a strong story.

Frame story – also known as a frame tale or nested narrative (frame narrative); the process of placing a story within a story to set the stage for other main events

Example: Canterbury Tales

Flashbacks in novels are frame stories, as well as prologues and epilogues.

Flash fiction – fiction that is extremely brief – usually only a few hundred words or fewer

Example: Hemingway's For *Whom the Bell Tolls* and *The Old Man and the Sea*

Feghoot – a type of short story with a pun or poetic joke (also known as a shaggy dog story)

As I wrote this blog post and researched this term, I wondered if this is where the phrase "you're a hoot" derived from.

Example: interior stories in Mark Twain's *Roughing It*

Fable – a story that uses animals, mythical creates, inanimate objects, or forces of nature to provide a moral

Example: Probably the most famous collection of fables is that of Aesop. (*The Lion and the Mouse, The Ant and the Grasshopper, etc.,*)

Drabble – similar to the mini saga but uses exactly 100 words, not including the title

Many examples of drabbles can be found here:

http://www.100wordstory.org/

Anecdote – a short, amusing encounter of a real person or event; a smaller part of a larger story

Example: two female friends in a novel, talking over lunch about something that happened to one of them on the way to the lunch date

Here are a few other terms used loosely to describe short fiction:

flash fiction
micro-fiction
micro-narrative
micro-story
postcard fiction
short story
sudden fiction
quick fiction
hint fiction
nano fiction

With so many ways to write fiction, writers have no more excuses! If you can't write a novel, try a short story. If you can't pen a short story, write an anecdote. Then another anecdote. Keep writing every day, and perhaps you can turn those anecdotes into a memoir of sorts.

Writing has never been so versatile, and we should take advantage of that!

TIP 316: Short treasures – more on short pieces

If you are working on your first book or feel you don't have a full-length novel inside of you, one way to get your writing and your name as an author into the world is to offer short stories. Many writing professionals simply call these "shorts" because they can include a multitude of writing pieces.

By sharing shorts, you allow your readers (and potential readers) to sample your writing talents in general, rather than limiting them to one specific genre.

Some examples of shorts are:

1. poetry

2. articles

3. character (or other) interviews

4. short stories / flash fiction

5. essays

6. reviews

7. fables

8. journal entries

9. monologues

10. short plays

11. songs

12. speeches

13. children's books or tall tales

14. excerpts

Many of the same writing practices of longer selections apply to shorts as well; the main difference is the length. Shorter pieces require the author to "get to the point" much sooner, as readers are expecting a quick payoff.

Rather than offering tips on writing short pieces, here are some writing prompts to get your juices flowing:

1. Put a twist (maybe even a dark one) on a favorite children's nursery rhyme or story.

2. They say everyone has a doppleganger (look alike). You've just met yours. How do you feel?

3. You've just been informed that you have three days to live. What do you do?

4. You and your teenager swap lives for a day? What happens?

5. You've just accomplished one of your life's goals. What is the goal? How do you feel?

6. You're in the bank and a robbery takes place. You're wearing a gun. Your kids are right beside you. What do you do?

7. Write a poem inspired by nature.

8. What would you say in a letter to your younger self?

9. A fugitive breaks into your home during the day while you and your kids are there. What do you do? How do you escape?

10. You take a trip to heaven or hell. What do you see?

11. You were involved in a horrendous auto accident and remain in a coma for two weeks. No one knows you can hear and remember everything going on around you, but you aren't able to respond. What do you experience while in the coma?

12. You get a chance to meet your country's leader (President). What do you talk about?

13. Write a poem or short story about your childhood.

14. You're an employee who is boss free for the day. What do you do?

15. You are a stay-home parent who is kid free for the day. What do you do?

16. Write about your first trip to the circus, a hockey game, a national landmark. What do you see, feel, hear, smell, and taste?

17. You're a five-year-old who gets lost at the local fair. What do you see, hear, feel?

18. You've been kidnapped. How do you escape?

19. You've been given the power to fly. Where do you go? How do you feel?

20. You've won a million dollars, but you MUST spend it all in one day. How do you spend it?

21. You overhear your best girlfriend talking to your husband in hushed tones. You can't make out exactly what they are saying, but you hear giggling. What are they talking about? What is the big secret?

22. You have an accident during which you hit your head. The doctor says you have amnesia. You don't remember being married to your spouse. Instead, you think you are married to your spouse's best friend, who happens to be single. What do you do?

23. Your pet can talk. What does it say?

24. Write about the worst day of your life.

25. Write about the best day of your life.

26. Write about the worst vacation you've ever had.

27. Write about the best vacation you've ever had.

28. You have a medical procedure performed that leaves you blind. The doctor says it will only last for three days. What do you do?

29. You are given one superpower for a day. What will it be?

30. You've been given the chance to go back in time and change one decision you've made. What do you change and why?

31. You have to live in the middle of nowhere without technology of any kind for one month. What do you do?

32. Describe your first real kiss.

33. You receive an all-expense-paid trip to any one place in the world. Where do you go?

34. Your teenage boys are home alone and you come home from work to see police cars lining your driveway. What happened?

35. You are lost in a strange city. What happens?

36. You get the chance to meet one celebrity. Who is it and why?

37. You get the chance to live someone else's life for one day. Who is it and why?

38. A deceased loved one visits you from beyond. Who is it and why?

39. Describe the ultimate marriage proposal.

40. You're at the park with your own kids one day and you see a two-year-old baby in a swing, all alone. There are no other adults around. What do you do?

41. You discover a secret passage in your house. Where does it lead? What do you discover?

42. Your parents share a huge secret with you on your eighteenth birthday, but it's not about you being adopted. What is the secret?

43. You are a videographer for a day. What do you film?

44. Rewrite a previously published piece in a different POV, perhaps that of a different gender or tense.

45. You're a ten-year-old child and your backyard playground transforms into a video game. Go!

46. You're on a public bus and as a stranger exits the bus, he passes you a piece of paper that contains an address and a picture of someone you know. What do you do?

47. You receive an anonymous phone call and a voice says, "I'm watching you," and the caller identifies you by your name. Who is tormenting you and why?

48. Every object in your house comes alive for a day! What do they say?

49. Write a short story or poem using nothing but clichés. Then rewrite it to eliminate the clichés but keep the same theme.

50. Literally vs. figuratively. For one day, everything you say or think comes to pass in real time. What happens?

51. You are given the chance to travel back into one famous moment in history. What moment do you choose? What happens?

I've provided fifty-one writing prompts here. If you've never written a "short" fiction or non-fiction piece, try it out. Shorts can be fun way to jump start your creativity. They may even turn into full-fledged stories if you are persistent.

Just for fun, here is a short fiction piece by Stephen Geez:

Sidekick

Short Fiction by Stephen Geez

www.StephenGeez.com

info@StephenGeez.com

I just figured out something all superheroes should know about our sidekicks.

I happened upon my own sidekick long before I grew up and stepped into the role of hero, way back when I was just a regular suburban kid with no inkling of my destiny as the savior of countless lives. Never a fan of those other heroes who star in their own comic books, I had no idea what a sidekick is supposed to do, let alone how much I would even need one.

And now, after decades working with my own sidekick for the common good, something has gone horribly wrong, and the blood is coming too fast, the injuries too severe, time too short. It's breaking my heart that our era as superhero and sidekick is about to end.

I was nine or ten years old when the world's most unlikely wannabe sidekick and his single-parent mom moved to our town. They set up housekeeping in that leaky rat's nest of an old farmhouse down the dirt road where overgrown fields pushed feebly against encroaching scrub. Two years younger than I, skinny and smallish for his age, he tried to look passable in tattered second-hand clothes usually sized too big or too small. Ever the bully magnet, he liked to pedal around on his chain-throwing rattletrap bicycle, a mismatch of old parts he'd scavenged. Since I was the only boy who didn't taunt him or push him down, he got to where he'd follow me about, hoping to join in while I hung out with others, but mostly content to hover at the periphery. He knew his place, but never acted resentful, instead appearing grateful for the tolerated proximity. No matter how much I ignored him, though, he often seemed to be watching me intently, studying me, as if appraising something only he could see.

Catching me alone with nowhere particular to go one day, he said he had a secret to tell me. He looked around as if worried someone might approach with bad intent. "Not here," he whispered.

Read more of this story by clicking here.

And here is one more if you're in the mood for something humorous.

A Match Met
By Beem Weeks

Nobody around these parts could ever recall a time when Charlie Tricklett had been anything less than fit as a proverbial fiddle. Even as a child, when every other kid in the fifth grade over at Sumpterville Elementary School let those Gawd-awful chicken pox come home to roost, amazing Charlie didn't find a single bump on his skin. So it became quite a curious thing when the man took to his sickbed late last month.

Now, nobody expected much would come of this rare bout with illness. It started right after Charlie had gone to bed one evening after his nightly pipe. He smoked out on his front porch, the way he'd done for most of his adult life. Next morning, though, the man complained of a busy stomach. Like maybe he'd ate a thing or two that didn't quite sit well with him.

"I'll get over this in a few hours," Charlie told his wife Elmira. "It ain't like I'm dying."

Elmira just gave up a short nod, handed the man his pipe, thus granting her approval for a rare indoor smoke.

Two days later old Charlie hadn't gotten any better. In fact, some might even say the man had taken a turn for the worse. He'd gone past vomiting, pushing up only air and a little spit from time to time. He didn't bother with food or drink, either; it'd only just have come right back up.

Two weeks into his ordeal Charlie sought the advice of Doctor Ronanberg—a rare occurrence indeed! The only time the good doctor ever entered the Tricklett home was on those once-monthly Friday night poker games.

Doc Ronanberg gave the man a thorough twice-over, gathering statistical details on things referred to as vitals, swiping a fair amount of blood and urine—of which old Charlie was none-too-pleased to part—before proclaiming the situation perplexing.

"Suppose it's some new plague," Charlie suggested to his wife. "Maybe they'll name it after me if I die from it."

"Doubtful," is all Elmira said of the subject, handing the man his nightly pipe.

* * *

The good people of Sumpterville took turns helping put Charlie's crops into his fields. The man himself couldn't so much as raise his head up off his pillow by that third week. But there'd be food on the table come harvest.

"Never could stand the smell of that awful poison," Charlie said, concerning the stink of herbicide coming off the freshly turned field next to the house. "Always makes me sick to my stomach."

* * *

By the end of the month, Charlie had reached his end. All the life had sneaked away during the previous weeks, leaving the man ready for his face-to-face with the Almighty.

It was here, on what would most certainly be his deathbed, that Charlie opted to ease his conscience, to make confession of what he'd been up to during that last month before he took sick.

Read more of this story by clicking here.

TIP 317: Tips for multi-genre authors

Many authors write in multiple genres, including sub-genres of fiction and nonfiction. Speaking as multi-genre author myself, I know it can be financially rewarding because it offers a multitude of income streams and can help you reach a variety of audiences, but it can also be quite time consuming.

You will want to keep your fiction and nonfiction titles separated most likely, because they are often very different audiences.

Here are 10 tips for writing and marketing in multiple genres:

1. Maintain separate social media accounts. Facebook pages can house all your writing if you wish. Twitter is a bit different because it uses hashtags, which are like little dividers that file your posts into categories or groups with those specific interests.

2. Create one blog, but set up different "pages" for each genre (fiction or nonfiction) you write – not per title, just genre. You can post excerpts or reviews per page per book.
    You can check mine out here: www.awordwithtraci.com

3. Target specific audiences per genre of books you write. This is the time-consuming part.

4. You can create multi-genre business cards:
    (Ex: Traci Sanders – author of parenting/children's/adult romance)
    or you can separate them and choose different fonts and

logos for each – non-fiction and fiction. The same would apply to your teasers and banners online.

5. Consider a pen name or a slightly different version of your real name to separate your fiction from nonfiction writing. I personally don't use a pen name. But I use Traci Sanders for my romance writing and Traci M. Sanders for my non-fiction and children's books.

6. Choose specific days to market your separate social media accounts. For instance, choose two days per week to only post on your fiction (or adult) account, and then two other days to post on your non-fiction (or children's) account. That's what I do. That way you're not flipping between accounts several times per day to keep up with posts.

7. Don't get bogged down with one book. The good thing about being a multi-genre author is that you are able to switch between books if you feel stuck on a certain chapter or topic.

8. Use keywords in your non-fiction titles. It helps the search engine find your books online.

9. Consider creating tutorial-type podcasts for your non-fiction work, especially for reference-type books.

10. Write your nonfiction books so that they read as engagingly as fiction, to exhibit your writing talent and style no matter which book of yours a reader chooses.

No matter which genre you are writing in at any given time, make sure to write with authenticity. For nonfiction, check your facts and cite any sources you use. For fiction, write in active voice and use descriptive details, as if painting your pages with words.

TIP 318: 11 ways to keep your stories going (sequels)

———— ❧ ————

Many times, an author publishes a novel and thinks, *What now? My character's story is over.* Sure, *that part* of the story is done, but it doesn't mean you have to stop there.

Here are 11 ways to keep your story going with the same theme/characters:

1. Create a story line in which the same main characters have gotten older (and hopefully wiser). For instance, if your original story involved a couple getting married and going through a hardship in the beginning of their lives together, focus on their life events as an older couple — perhaps as grandparents. Maybe they see their grown children going through hardships.

2. If a couple has young children in your first book, tell the second story from the POV of the main characters' children as adults.

3. Write a spin-off story about a secondary character from your first book: perhaps a best friend, a man or woman with whom a main character had an affair in the first book, a sibling, a parent or child, or even an arch enemy of a main character—to tell another side of the story. Many times, readers connect even more strongly with secondary characters than main ones and want to know more about them.

4. Keep a life story going. If in the first book your couple gets married but doesn't have children, make the second story about their lives as young parents, or perhaps they suffer the loss of one of their children.

5. Use the same main characters and create a different setting. They could move to an exotic city across the world and face new challenges.

6. Create a story where a main character from the first book dies but is able to connect with his or her spouse or loved one from the beyond in the second book. This would work well if your first book left an opening for the story to keep going.

7. If in the first book, there was a gap of time that could be filled in as Book 1.5 instead of Book 2, perhaps a novella, such as what a main character did while a loved one was in a coma, or if the couple had a "break" during their relationship. What *really* went on during that period of time?

8. If the first book is about an adult character, make the second book a "How it all began ..." type of story to tell something tragic or compelling that happened in that character's childhood which would tie in with their demeanor and personality in the first book, or fill in an important piece of the story.

9. In the second book, create a skeleton from a first-book character's past—perhaps an arch enemy from childhood who tries to destroy his/her professional or personal life. Or it could be a first love who wants the main character back, or a child a character never knew he had.

10. If your first story ended happily or was a light-hearted tale throughout, create a tragedy or hardship in your subsequent story—same characters, maybe one or two new ones added. Remember, characters are flexible, alterable. Life events can change a person—make him or her bitter, sad, happy, adopt an addiction, etc.

11. Create a previously un-mentioned or un-discovered family secret in the second book—perhaps a wife confesses to her husband that their child isn't his biological child, or maybe it is revealed during a life-threatening situation.

Don't feel that just because your first story ended happily that there is nothing more to tell. Characters are like clay entities and, as authors, we are the molders of that clay. We can manipulate our characters into whatever we'd like. We can add more clay (more characters), take some away (kill characters), or flatten it all out and start anew (complete a whole new story line with different characters). The power is in our hands!

**Bonus tip: Many authors are doing stand-alone series these days that include the same theme throughout but with different characters. That is always an option.

After You Publish Part 6
Managing the Media

TIP 319: How to build an author portfolio – media package

At some point in your career as an author, you will be participating in some type of social media event. Therefore, you will want to have what is called a "media kit" at the ready.

This is a Word document which includes important information about you and your writing.

Here is a list of the items you may want to include in your media kit:

- professional-quality (candid or serious) photo of yourself – readers and other authors like to connect faces to names.

- short author bio – be sure to include what genre(s) you write in

- book covers – for any books you wish to promote

- book buy links

- Amazon author page link

- book blurbs

- book excerpts

- author contact links – for all social media platforms (you never know where you will meet your next loyal fan)

- website or blog link

- links to any book trailers on YouTube

Be sure to hyperlink the links where appropriate so the blogger/host of the party simply has to copy and paste everything into his or her program or site. Make it as easy as possible on your hosts. They are doing you a favor.

Your author media kit is much like a portfolio (for an artist or model). It's what represents your work, and you in general. Take the time to ensure it's as professional as possible.

TIP 320: Public speaking

At some point in your writing career, you may be asked to give a speech in front of a crowd. Some people would rather cut off their right arm than have to speak in public but, sometimes, requests for speeches arise without much warning.

Perhaps you will be asked to offer a reading of one of your books, thank a committee for an award you receive, or interview on radio or television.

Regardless of the reason for your speech, here are a few tips that will help you deliver your words with confidence.

1. Practice your speech a few times in front of the mirror (if time allows). Take note of your body language. Also, practice in front of a few friends. Ask them for pointers. But don't practice so much that you drive yourself crazy.

2. Take a few deep breaths before you go on stage or in front of the audience.

3. Don't forget to smile, even if no one else in the audience does.

4. Once you step up to the microphone or podium, pause and gather your thoughts (and your courage) before you start speaking.

5. Smile and relax as much as possible.

6. It's okay to have notes jotted down, to glance at occasionally, but make sure you don't keep your eyes glued to the paper and risk avoiding the audience.

7. Make eye contact with various individuals in the crowd, especially those who seem to be smiling (receptive) to you. It will help you relax.

8. Have a sense of humor. Be human and personable.

9. Try not to talk with your hands.

10. Monitor your speed. Try not to rush through it. Pause in between every few sentences.

11. Remember that the people in the audience are probably just as terrified of speaking in public as you are. Everyone gets jitters at some point in their lives. Many famous singers claim to get jitters before they go on stage, whether they've done it a handful of times or have been performing for years. Part of the nervousness is excitement and adrenaline, so enjoy yourself.

12. Thank everyone for coming and supporting you. A brief, "Thank you" or "Thank you for your time" will suffice.

Just remember, your life doesn't depend on that speech. As long as you don't take it too seriously, and just relax and try to connect with your audience, you will get through it.

TIP 321: Capitalizing on media appearances

A good friend of mine, top Amazon reviewer and well-respected author—Gisela Hausmann—has written several books about how to promote yourself on television and radio stations. She's appeared as an expert on email marketing several times in her local area.

If you are an author who would like to learn exactly how to go about approaching television or radio producers, I highly suggest you get her book and learn from the best. I just bought this book a week ago and already have gotten two positive responses about projects (articles I have submitted) for prominent magazines. These tips work! She even offers 100 pitches to use.

https://www.amazon.com/BOOK-MARKETING-Funnel-Including-Pitches/dp/0996897275/ref=sr_1_1?ie=UTF8&qid=148687222 2&sr=8-1&keywords=gisela+hausmann

I'm going to share just one tip she was gracious enough to impart on me recently: blog features count as media appearances, just like television and radio spots.

When your work is featured anywhere, take advantage of that publicity and add it to your blog.

Create a page on your blog titled something like "In the News" or "My Appearances" or "Media Room" – something to get your readers' attention. Then, go to the blogs or websites where your work is featured and do a "screenshot" of each one. Post them on your media page on your own blog. Even pictures from your latest book signing can be included on your media page.

Once this is created, potential readers, publishers, or agents can view your media experience to vet you for spots with their entities. When you have a television appearance, take a screen shot of it as well and post it as an image on your media page.

If you happen to have video footage of your appearances, definitely post those on your blog. Videos are huge sales tools. People feel more connected with you when they can match a voice and personality to a face.

If you look at the top of my home page at www.awordwithtraci.com, you will see a tab that says, "In the News."

Click on it to check out my latest radio interview if you'd like. You will also see some of the blogs I've been featured on. My point in sharing this with you is to show you how a media page could be set up.

TIP 322: Tips for radio interviews

Many authors, especially those who write reference-type books, seek out opportunities to be featured on media outlets to promote their work. Or they may be contacted by local newspaper staff or television stations to be featured.

If you've ever been on the radio, you know how nerve-wrecking it can be. You worry you will stutter or draw a blank with your words, or that you will say something stupid. It's a bit more challenging than in-person interviews because you aren't sitting in front of that person, watching his/her body language. You can only "guess" how you are being perceived by the person by the inflection of his/her voice. You don't have those visual cues that let you know when it's your turn to speak.

With the help of technology, many radio shows can be conducted from the privacy of the host's and/or guest's home these days. While no radio interview will be perfect—thing can happen that are beyond your control—there are some steps you can take to prepare yourself.

Here are 13 things you can do to have a successful radio interview:

1. Make sure you know the name of the radio station you are being featured on and the radio show host's name.

2. Jot down a few notes of things you might want to talk about. Most of the time, the show host sends you a list of questions you may be asked.

3. Listen to what the host is saying/asking you during the interview to ensure you offer an intelligible and intelligent

answer. Wait two seconds after the host stops speaking before you answer so you can gather your thoughts, and to make sure you don't accidentally interrupt the host or talk over him/her.

4. Try to pay attention to your answers to ensure you aren't repeating the same phrases or words. I did a radio show recently where all of my answers were intelligent, my voice sounded great, I was engaging and the host seemed to have fun interviewing me, but I continuously said the word "absolutely" – like 8000 times in that one interview (or at least it sounded that way in my head when I later listened to it).

5. Take your time answering questions. Be friendly and engaging; be yourself. Don't try to use big words to sound intelligent, or try to change your voice to be someone you aren't. The host wants to interview *you*! The listeners want to get to know the real you.

6. If you have a link, image, or at the very least, a day and time with information about your upcoming interview, be sure to share it on social media several days before the show to draw listeners in. Some may listen in simply in hopes of hearing you screw it up; others will do so to be genuinely supportive of you.

7. The radio show host will give you instructions as to what to do if your call is disconnected. The majority of the time, he/she will tell you to stand by and wait for the call back—especially live shows.

8. If you are taking call-ins, be friendly, open, honest, and thank them for calling in, even if they are only trying to bash you. Simply say something like, "I appreciate you taking a chance on my books. I realize they aren't for everyone," and leave it at that.

9. Be sure to repeat your plugs periodically, for the listeners who drop in and out of the show, or join late. Don't be annoying or pushy about it, but do mention your book titles a few times. Usually the host will do that for you, though.

10. Be sure to offer ways the listeners can find out more about you and your work. Social media accounts, website links, blog links, and your pen name (if applicable).

11. Make sure your space is quiet and non-distracting during the interview. If you are at home, conduct the interview in a separate room with the door locked to avoid background noise. I have even done radio interviews in my car. It's very quiet in there.

12. Practice in front of a friend or record yourself to practice a few days before the interview. Try to avoid words like "um, yeah, totally, like, honestly, or literally." Also, make sure to keep curse words out of your interview.

13. Be sure to thank the listeners, the radio station, and the host before ending the interview.

I hope these tips will come in handy during your next radio interview. I will be offering a separate post on tips for live or in-person media interviews later. Certain things pertain to those, compared to radio interviews, such as "smiling for the camera." Smiling can apply to radio interviews as well though. Listeners can detect tone in your voice and, if you are smiling, chances are, your tone is friendly and inviting.

**Bonus tip: Drink a few sips of wine to relax before the interview. It really helps.

TIP 323: How to get on TV

Since I don't have a great deal of personal experience with television interviews, I am pleased to have a fellow author friend Gisela Hausmann here to offer valuable advice on this topic. She has appeared on TV many times discussing strategies for effective emailing as well as how to obtain reviews on Amazon. She is known as the "email Guru" in the author community.

Her work has been featured in the SUCCESS magazine. She has appeared on WYFF-TV4, her local TV-station, four times in the last six months. Gisela graduated with a master's degree in Film and mass media from the University of Vienna; she has produced dozens of features for TV.

http://www.giselahausmann.com/newsroom.html
Here is an excerpt from her highly acclaimed book *Naked News for Indie Authors: How to Get on TV*.

(Update: this particular book is no long available by this author; however, she has a wonderful new book out that includes 100 ready-made media pitches. I highly recommend it.)

https://www.amazon.com/BOOK-MARKETING-Funnel-Including-Pitches/dp/0996897275/ref=sr_1_1?ie=UTF8&qid=148687222 2&sr=8-1&keywords=gisela+hausmann

* * *

WHY, AND HOW, TO PITCH TV-ANCHORS/ STATIONS

Marketing experts tell us that, on average, buyers have to see a new product or hear about it seven times before they buy. Buyers want reassurances from various sources, that they'll be buying a great product. People listen to family members, friends, Facebook friends, tweeps, newspaper reporters, magazine writers, and TV-anchors.

Among these various sources, TV has a special role. Getting featured on TV allows authors to charge higher prices and also to get paid speaking engagements.

The simple truth is that the more often we see somebody on TV, the more likely we think that this person is somebody whose work we need to check out.

People who give tips on TV or who comment on current events are considered to be *experts* in their fields. People who are featured on TV very often achieve celebrity status (locally or nationally). They create buzz for their work.

In short, there are three reasons why you should consider working on getting media coverage:

- people like to buy experts' books (locally and nationally)

- experts can charge more for their books

- known experts have it much easier to get speaking engagements

Unfortunately, many authors think that TV is reserved for nonfiction authors, but that's not true. It is only natural that an author who wrote a historical romance novel knows a lot about romance in historic times e.g., the Middle Ages.

Similarly, a writer of historic novels set in the South of the United States can talk about

- The 80th Anniversary of the publication of *Gone With the Wind* is coming up (June 10, 2016). Why are people still fascinated with historic novels about the South and will always be!

Sci-fi authors can pitch the media every year shortly before July 8, the day on which the Roswell incident gets commemorated.

Horror authors can take advantage of Halloween and Frankenstein Day (August 30).

Notice that a 30-year-old anchor probably has no clue that this anniversary is coming up and most likely will react with, "Oh, I love this 'expert'! That's great and totally new idea for a news feature."

Pitching the media is nothing else but relating "your topic" to seasonal or current events.

So, how do you get on TV?

Naturally, "Good Morning America" and "The Ellen DeGeneres Show" aren't waiting for you, but local TV anchors are.

Here is a fact not too many people know. Though anchors are experts in presenting the news, they cannot *interpret* the news because that would be biased. For instance, if a suicide bomber blows himself up in a crowded location in the Middle East, anchors cannot speculate about the consequences of this attack but they would love to hear from a veteran, who has served in this area (and who may have also penned a book about his experiences).

To get on TV:

1. Firstly, analyze *your topic* (not your book).

2. Play an association game with yourself: How does your topic relate to current events, upcoming holidays, general trends, new gadgets, and products that are "in"? Unlike books, TV deals only with the here and the now.

3. Acquire any knowledge you may be missing.

4. Pitch your idea in bullet points to the morning show anchor(s) of your local TV-station (ABC, CBS, and NBC are better than FOX. FOX prefers syndicated content.) Mention the words "local author" in your subject line so anchors are aware that you are available on short notice.

5. If the anchor does not call you back, follow up with a phone call two days later.

6. Call about 15 minutes after this anchor's show has ended, and begin your phone call by introducing yourself and asking if this is a good minute to talk.

7. Sound confident and work your case. If the anchor does not like your exact topic, ask if he/ she would like you to pitch a variation.

8. Speak slowly and be composed so the anchor can imagine that you'll be good on TV.

9. If the anchor invites you: Prepare!

10. Rehearse – rehearse – rehearse your topic in sound bites – in front of a big mirror. Watch your hands – Don't move them too much.

11. Before or after the show ask the anchor to send you a link to the clip as featured on the TV-station's webpage.

12. Pull a screen-print and pin it on your website, your Amazon author page, and everywhere else where you can feature it.

13. To succeed, always remember – Do NOT pitch your book! Pitch your "expert knowledge." The TV-anchor will be happy to mention your book for you.

If you still wonder if you should attempt to get on TV, just think – "Kardashians"!

They are on TV, which is pretty much all they do; still Khloe's book is ranked #4,770 Paid in Kindle Store and acquired 322 customer reviews in 5 1/2 months, at a price of $12.99 (for the Kindle edition).

Hope to see your TV clip on the web soon!

* * *

I want to thank Gisela Hausmann again for sharing this guest post with us about television appearances. I've learned a great deal about marketing from her. Be sure to check out all her books on Amazon!

Conclusion

We've come to the end of our journey together in this book series. You've been offered 365 tips on various aspects of the publishing process from grammar and editing, to creating compelling characters and stories, and ending with marketing and networking.

I don't pretend to know everything about the publishing industry, not even close. But I have done an extensive amount of research on the topics I discussed in these books, and I have put many of them to practice in my own publishing endeavors, with great success.

Thank you for joining me on this journey, and I wish you much success in your own publishing adventures!

I also write parenting, children's, and romance titles. Feel free to check them out on my Amazon page here:

https://www.amazon.com/Traci-M.-Sanders/e/B00BA9VUUY/ref=sr_ntt_srch_lnk_4?qid=1486343706&sr=1-4

If you enjoy the books in this series, I'd be ever so grateful if you'd share your thoughts in the form of a review on Amazon, Goodreads, and any other social media sites you deem appropriate, to help other authors find them.

~Reviews keep authors writing!~

Special thanks

Special thanks to the following authors for their contributions to this book: (in no particular order)

- Stephen Geez
- Beem Weeks
- Mark Fine
- Beth Hale
- Gisela Hausmann
- Sharon K. Connell

Thanks to everyone who followed my blog segment in 2016 and for hanging with me in my video-blog segment for 2017, where I offer tips on how to balance your writing time and personal time.

Find me on YouTube:

https://www.youtube.com/channel/UCSa4YNcX4DOvqMQge Uhj_VA